BUSINESS *the*

Jack Welch

Welch **Way**

BUSINESS the

Way

10 Secrets of the World's Greatest Turnaround King

By Stuart Crainer

AMACOM

American Management Association

New York • Atlanta • Boston • Chicago • Kansas City • San Francisco • Washington, D.C.

Brussels • Mexico City • Tokyo • Toronto

Business the Jack Welch Way was written independently by the author, Stuart Crainer. It has not been authorized by its subject.

This publication is designed to provide accurate and authoritative information in regard to the subject matter covered. It is sold with the understanding that the publisher is not engaged in rendering legal, accounting, or other professional service. If legal advice or other expert assistance is required, the services of a competent professional person should be sought.

Library of Congress Cataloging-in-Publication Data
Crainer, Stuart.
   Business the Jack Welch way: ten secrets of the world's greatest
turnaround king / Stuart Crainer.
      p.   cm.
   Includes bibliographical references and index.
   ISBN 0-8144-7033-5
      1. Welch, Jack (John Francis), 1935-   . 2. General Electric
Company—Management.   3. Chief executive officers—United States—
Biography.   4. Industrial management—United States.
5. Leadership—United States.   I. Title.
HD9697.A3U534   1999
658.4'063—dc21   98-50489
                                                                        CIP

Published in North America by arrangement with Capstone
Publishing Limited, Oxford, United Kingdom.

Printing number

10   9   8   7   6   5   4   3   2

Contents

One: Invest in People   23

People matter. Talking to them and meeting them takes up a serious chunk of Jack Welch's time. So, too, does developing people for the future. He talks, pontificates, cajoles and educates. But, most of all, he connects.

Two: Dominate Your Market ... or Get Out   35

The choice is simple and is repeatedly laid out by Jack Welch. He has no time for companies that are fourth or fifth in their market. He wants to be first or a close second. Gain market leadership and take the market by the scruff of the neck and lead it forward. If you can't get to the front, sell the business and look elsewhere.

Three: Never Sit Still   43

Jack Welch is restless. Despite heart surgery, he never stops. He has inculcated GE with the same sort of restless energy. The company won't stay still or rest on its laurels. GE changes and then changes again. It is always nearer its goals by never staying in one place.

Four: Think Service   61

Pre-Welch, GE was a manufacturer, a good old-fashioned champion of the smokestacks. Welch introduced it to service. Now GE is a service company that also manufactures. It is a finance company and an information company as well as a maker of appliances. Quality and service link its activities.

For a company with such a great history, GE under Welch has become preoccupied with the future. It embraces the new—whether it be IT or the Internet. Welch envisions the future. He speaks enthusiastically about the future. And GE creates the future.

The new model leader is not a corporate dictator. The leader is committed to learning, deciding and moving forward. Wrong decisions present their own opportunities. Learning from failure is more important than wallowing in success.

Jack Welch communicates. He is straight. Whether he is talking to workers in a GE factory, managers on a training program or industry analysts, he speaks with passionate clarity. He tells it as it is.

Dismayed by the time-wasting of bureaucracy and hierarchy, Jack Welch nearly left GE after his first year. He was talked into staying, but the bugbear remained. Since taking over at the top, Welch has eradicated bureaucracy with a vengeance.

The corporate person is supposedly dead. But Jack Welch has done all right sticking with a single employer. How has he managed to learn and develop in a single organization?

Jack Welch manages GE as if it were a corner store. The same things matter: quality and service; cash flow; keeping abreast of what sells, what part of the business is doing well; people. The fact that you are selling nuclear power plants and not candy bars is immaterial.

Preface

The management gurus tell us that in the contemporary business world learning is a source of competitive advantage. Managers must constantly learn new skills and techniques so that they are armed for corporate battle. Organizations must reinvent themselves as learning organizations in which learning is central to their being and culture. All this is no doubt true—in theory. But, in reality, there are few genuine learning organizations. The reality is that executives are not very good at learning. "Success in the marketplace increasingly depends on learning, yet most people don't know how to learn. What's more, those members of the organization that many assume to be the best at learning are, in fact, not very good at it," says Harvard Business School's Chris Argyris.[1] One of the aims of this series is to help executives learn; to give them the opportunity to learn from the best.

This may sound an overly ambitious objective. But think how managers learn. First, they do so through experience. Yet, as Chris Argyris has pointed out, experience is no guarantee of learning. How many executives have you met who have all the experience in the world but little insight or real wisdom? They may proclaim that they have 30 years' experience, but they often have one year's experience 30 times. Experience does not automatically lead to learning. Years clocked up do not necessarily equate with wisdom.

The second source of learning for executives is training programs. Most senior managers have attended one business school executive program or another.

With their case studies and emphasis on the analytical, business schools undoubtedly enable managers to acquire important skills. But the range of skills and their practical usefulness is regularly questioned— not least by those who teach at business schools. "The idea that you can take smart but inexperienced 25-year-olds who have never managed anything or anybody and turn them into effective managers via two years of classroom training is ludicrous," says strategy guru Henry Mintzberg.[2]

The venerable Peter Drucker is another longtime critic of business schools. "The business schools in the U.S., set up less than a century ago, have been preparing well-trained clerks," he wrote as long ago as 1969.[3]

Business schools remain wedded to theory; business is about action.

More recently, he has predicted the decline of business schools, noting that "Business schools are suffering from premature success. Now, they are improving yesterday a little bit. The worst thing is to improve what shouldn't be done at all."

Business schools remain wedded to theory; business is about action. "I am not impressed by diplomas. They don't do the work. My marks were not as good as those of others, and I didn't take the final examination. The principal called me in and said I have to leave. I told him that I didn't want a diploma. They had less value than a cinema ticket. A ticket at least guaranteed that you would get in. A diploma guaranteed nothing," said Soichiro Honda, founder of Honda.[4]

With surprising understatement, former Chrysler CEO Lee Iacocca noted: "Formal learning can teach you a great deal, but many of the essential skills in life are the ones you have to develop on your own." More opinionated was the late Avis chief and author of *Up the Organization*, Robert Townsend. "Don't hire Harvard Business School graduates," he warned. "This elite, in my opinion, is missing some pretty fundamental requirements for success: humility; respect for people in the firing line; deep understanding of the nature of the business and the kind of people who can enjoy themselves making it prosper; respect from way down the line; a demonstrated record of guts, industry, loyalty down, judgment, fairness, and honesty under pressure."[5]

More recently, Bill Gates, Virgin's Richard Branson and Body Shop's Anita Roddick have all been much quoted examples of those who missed out on business school but went on to reach the summits of business success. "A great advantage I had when I started the Body Shop was that I had never been to business school," says Anita Roddick. Similarly, 1-800-Flowers founder Jim McCann says that the company would have not got off the ground if he'd gone to business school—"I would have thought too much about why the deal couldn't be done," says McCann.[6]

The third source of learning is learning from peers and colleagues. This is very powerful. The current trend for mentoring and coaching is evidence that senior managers can play an important role in developing the skills of other, more junior, managers. But, what if your boss is an ineffective time-server with no interest in developing tomorrow's talent? What if your boss is incompetent? What if your aspirations far outstrip the level of expertise of your boss? Who do you learn from then?

For many, the answer lies in the growing array of bestselling books by corporate leaders. Executives buy them in their millions. They want to know what makes a top CEO tick. They want it mapped out. Invariably they are disappointed. Most CEO authored books are marred by ego and hindsight. They are ghostwritten and their merit is as illusory as a ghost. Most are rose-tinted celebrations of careers rather than objective examinations of managerial techniques. The learning they offer is limited—though that is not to deny the entertainment value.

The Big Shots series aims to fill the gap. It seeks to give an objective view of the business practice and thinking of some of the corporate greats. For each of the business leaders in the series—whether it be Bill Gates, Rupert Murdoch, Richard Branson or Jack Welch—we look at the essence of their approach to business. What makes them different? What are they good at? And, most importantly, what lessons can be learned from their business success?

As you will see, the lessons aren't rocket science. Indeed, management is more pocket science. Theory is for those with time on their hands. "We don't claim to be the global fountainhead of management thought, but we may be the world's thirstiest pursuer of big ideas—from whatever their source—and we're not shy about adopting and adapting them," says Jack Welch.[7] Make the best ideas your own because there is no single, all-embracing big idea. Making it happen is what management and business are all about. Ask Jack Welch.

NOTES

1 Argyris, Chris, "Teaching smart people how to learn," *Harvard Business Review*, May–June 1991.

2 Mintzberg, Henry, "The new management mind-set," *Leader to Leader*, Spring 1997.

3 Drucker, Peter, *The Age of Discontinuity*, Heinemann, London, 1969.

4 Crainer, Stuart (editor), *The Ultimate Book of Business Quotations*, Capstone, Oxford, 1997; AMACOM, New York, 1998.

5 Townsend, Robert, *Up the Organization* (out of print).

6 Bruce, Katherine, "How to succeed in business without an MBA," *Forbes*, January 26, 1998.

7 Letter to shareholders, February 1993.

The Life and Times of Jack Welch

John Francis Welch, Junior was born on November 19, 1935 in Peabody, Massachusetts. His father was a conductor on the Boston & Maine Railroad, his mother a housewife. When Welch went to the University of Massachusetts to study chemical engineering, he was the first one from his family to go to college. Explaining his choice of subject, Welch has said: "I had an uncle who was an engineer at a power station in Salem, so an engineer was something. I took chemistry and fell in love with chemistry. And chemistry and engineering went together."[1]

It is notable that engineering holds a strong fascination for industrialists and those who think about business. "I'm an engineer by training—and disposition," admits Tom Peters (who trained as a civil engineer at Cornell and later built bridges in Vietnam).[2] Harvard Business School's Michael Porter is an aeronautical engineer; the former McKinsey strategist Kenichi Ohmae is a nuclear physicist and Henry

Mintzberg a trained engineer. Mintzberg has robustly attacked Wall Street and financiers—"These are the people most distant from the ones who make, sell, use, and service a product, but because they have the financial training they control a company"—and noted with wry pleasure that corporate titans such as Welch and Intel's Andy Grove are engineers by training, willing to get their hands dirty.[3] Taking things apart and understanding how they work remains Welch's instinct.

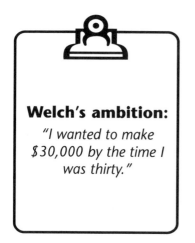

Welch's ambition:

"I wanted to make $30,000 by the time I was thirty."

Welch went on to study for a PhD in chemical engineering at the University of Illinois. When he left the university, Welch recalls that, "I wanted to make $30,000 by the time I was thirty."[4]

He then joined GE's plastics division at Pittsfield, Massachusetts in 1960. The attractions of GE were that it was near his family's Massachusetts home and the lure of the salary: $10,500. The imagined status of a $30,000 salary had to wait a little longer.

Welch did not fall in love with GE at first sight. After a year, he tried to leave his job at Pittsfield to join International Minerals & Chemicals in Skokie, Illinois. The youthful, headstrong Welch was frustrated by what he saw as corporate bureaucracy. Welch was talked into staying. His boss promised to get the bureaucracy off his back. (He did, but Welch has raged against bureaucracy ever since.)

Welch then began a speedy and spectacular climb up the GE hierarchy. In 1968, at the age of 33, he became GE's youngest general manager. Then he became senior vice president and sector executive for the consumer products and services sector as well as vice chairman of the GE Credit Corporation. By 1979 he was vice chairman and executive officer. Along the way he built plastics into a formidable $2 billion business; turned around the medical diagnostics business; and began the development of GE Capital. His touch was sure.

The final leap to the uppermost reaches of the GE hierarchy came in 1977 when GE chairman Reg Jones suggested Welch move to headquarters at Fairfield, Connecticut to join in the race to succeed him. Jones knew what he was looking for in his successor. Pretty soon he recognized that Welch fitted the bill.

"We need entrepreneurs who are willing to take well-considered business risks—and at the same time know how to work in harmony with a larger business entity," said Jones, a man honest enough to recognize his own limitations. "The intellectual requirements are light-years beyond the requirements of less complex organizations."[5]

The CEO's job description:

"We need entrepreneurs who are willing to take well-considered business risks—and at the same time know how to work in harmony with a larger business entity."

This is not to suggest that Jones' decision was made on the spot. Indeed, he began thinking about his successor in 1974 and came up with an initial shortlist of nearly 100 top-performing GE executives. This was reduced to six who reported directly to the Corporate Executive Office. The six included Welch. "The management-succession process that placed venerable General Electric in Welch's hands exemplifies the best and most vital aspects of the old GE culture," wrote Noel Tichy and Stratford Sherman. "Jones insisted on a long, laborious, exactingly thorough process that would carefully consider every eligible candidate, then rely on reason alone to select the best qualified. The result ranks among the finest examples of succession planning in corporate history."[6]

In December 1980, Welch was announced as the new CEO and chairman of GE. It was a record-breaking appointment. At 45, Welch was the youngest chief the company had ever appointed. Indeed, he was only the eighth CEO the company had appointed in 92 years.

He took over a company that was a model for American corporate might and for modern management techniques. GE had moved with the times—though usually more slowly. It got there eventually but was, even then, a sizable juggernaut. Changing direction and learning new tricks weren't things that came naturally. GE was in the habit of weighing things up, then moving, minimizing risks but still progressing forward. It was highly focused but still managed to view the world more broadly than some other corporate giants.

When Jack Welch became top man GE's net income was $1.7 billion. By most measures, the company was growing at a healthy rate—by nine percent in the previous year. Everything seemed rosy. More plain sailing was anticipated as the new chief got used to the job. After all, Welch was an insider. He was hardly likely to turn on the organization that had nurtured him so carefully. Was he?

GE CHIEFS AND THE GE WAY

But what sort of company was Jack Welch taking over? GE was—and is—one of the great corporate stories. It has survived the vicissitudes of time with remarkable resilience.

In 1878, Thomas A. Edison set up the Edison Electric Light Company. The company evolved into the Edison General Electric Company and, in 1892, merged with Thomson-Houston Electric Company to form the General Electric Company. In 1896, when the Dow Jones Industrial Index was launched, General Electric was listed. It is the only one of the original companies still listed.

Indeed, companies may be legal entities, but they are disturbingly mortal. "The natural average lifespan of a corporation should be as long as two or three centuries," writes Arie de Geus in *The Living Company*, noting a few prospering relics such as the Sumitomo Group and the Scandinavian company, Stora.[7] However, the reality is that companies do not head off into the Florida sunset to play bingo. They usually die young. GE is an exception—a very large exception.

De Geus quotes a Dutch survey of corporate life expectancy in Japan and Europe that came up with 12.5 years as the average life expectancy of all firms. "The average life expectancy of a multinational corporation—Fortune 500 or its equivalent—is between 40 and 50 years," says de Geus, noting that one-third of 1970's Fortune 500 had disappeared by 1983. Such endemic failure is attributed by de Geus to the focus of managers on profits and the bottom line rather than on the human community that makes up their organization.

In an attempt to get to the bottom of this mystery, de Geus and a number of his Shell colleagues carried out some research to identify the characteristics of corporate longevity. As you would expect, the onus is on keeping excitement to a minimum, being more like Ronald Reagan than James Dean. The average human centurion advocates a life of abstinence, caution and moderation, and so it is with companies. The Royal Dutch/Shell team identified four key characteristics of long-lived companies. They were "sensitive to their environment"; "cohesive, with a strong sense of identity"; "tolerant"; and "conservative in financing." (These conclusions are echoed in Jerry Porras and James Collins' equally thought provoking, *Built to Last*, which almost serves as a companion volume to de Geus' book.)

Key to de Geus' entire argument is that there is more to companies—and to longevity—than mere money making. "The dichotomy between profits and longevity is false," he says. His logic is impeccably straightforward. Capital is no longer king; the skills, capabilities and knowledge of people are. The corollary to this is that "a successful company is one that can learn effectively." Learning is tomorrow's capital. In de Geus' eyes, learning means being prepared to accept continuous change.

De Geus would like GE. Its progression has, indeed, been built on solid foundations. It earned $3 million in its first seven months of existence and has been run cautiously and prudently ever since. One generation has handed control on to another seamlessly. All have been committed to change, to a greater or lesser extent. "GE's genius has been in its choice of successive CEOs each of whom tended to counter the extremes of his predecessors," concluded Richard Pascale after studying the company's history.[8]

Indeed, the performance of GE's CEOs has been consistently good. In their book *Built to Last*, Jerry Porras and Jim Collins found that Welch's record in his first decade in charge wasn't the best in GE's history. In fact, the celebrated CEO came in fifth place out of seven when measured by return on equity. "To have a Welch-cal-

"To have a century of Welch-caliber CEOs all grown from inside— well, that is one key reason why GE is a visionary company."

iber CEO is impressive. To have a century of Welch-caliber CEOs all grown from inside—well, that is one key reason why GE is a visionary company," conclude Porras and Collins.[9] It is a formidable record. No other large organization has been so successful in recruiting from within or managed to sustain such exceptional performance over such an extended period.

Another reason behind GE's success is that it has been built around a simple, common-sense culture. Nothing fancy has distracted it, no thrills, nothing too smart. "Sure we have good people, but we were all taken from the same pool as the people of all other companies, and yet I think we have something unique," ex-CEO Fred Borch said in 1965. "And our uniqueness, I think, is due to this matter of climate; respect for one another and working at our jobs to have as much darn fun out of it as we possibly can."[10]

Keeping it simple means that GE goes through CEOs at a far slower rate than its rivals. As Don Hambrick and Greg Fukotoni pointed out in 1991, since 1960 some 19 percent of CEO's in Fortune 500s served for less than three years.[11] GE, on the other hand, is rarely on the phone to headhunters. GE has long recognized that it is better and cheaper to nurture talent and promote from within. It is significant that GE executives are enthusiastically courted by other companies.

The roll call of GE CEOs is:

- **Charles Coffin.** Chairman and CEO from 1892-1922, Coffin was the leader of the group that bought Edison's patents and began the serious development of the business.

- **Gerard Swope.** Swope joined GE in 1919 as the first president of International General Electric. He became president in 1922 with Owen Young as chairman. By the late 1920s the company had 75,000 employees and sales of $300 million. The company moved into home appliances. Swope emphasized the company's heritage as an engineering and manufacturing company, and combined that with solid systems and, by the standards of the times, progressive human resources management. The Swope Plan of 1931 was one of the building blocks of the New Deal. Swope retired in 1939 but returned temporarily when his successor was appointed to wartime jobs.

- **Charles Wilson.** Wilson's tenure from 1940 until 1952 was interrupted by wartime work, which made his impact and legacy less substantial than those of his predecessors.

- **Ralph Cordiner.** Cordiner was GE's CEO from 1950 until 1963. He was a robust champion of decentralization, which necessitated the creation of complex bureaucratic systems. His unsettling years in charge were notable for the introduction of Management by Objectives, a concept fashioned by a bright young management thinker named Peter Drucker who worked closely with the company at the time. Cordiner also launched GE Plastics and the company's aircraft engines businesses. He set up the company's Crotonville training center. Cordiner emphasized marketing and developed a new corporate slogan: "Progress is our most important product." His book, *New Frontiers for Professional Managers* (1956), summarized his managerial philosophy.

- **Fred Borch.** Borch introduced GE to strategic planning and calmed things down a little from the Cordiner years. His impact is favorably recalled by Jack Welch: "Borch let a thousand flowers bloom. He got us into modular housing and entertainment businesses, nurtured GE Credit through its infancy, embarked on ventures in Europe, and let Aircraft Engine and Plastics alone so they could really get started. It became evident after he stepped down that General Electric had once again established a foothold into some businesses with a future."[12] Borch ruled the GE roost from 1964 until 1972.

- **Reg Jones.** British-born Jones joined GE in 1939. In 1967 he became Chief Financial Officer and was named CEO in 1973. Jones developed GE's business in high-tech markets such as jet engines and nuclear reactors, as well as sharpening up its financial systems. He was voted the U.S.'s most influential executive in 1979 and CEO of the year in 1980. A former GE executive later commented: "During Jones' tenure, GE was financially strong but it was a dull, unexciting company. We were an organization in decline—and that was not recognized."[13] Jones' diligent succession planning led to Jack Welch, CEO.

STAGE ONE: NEUTRON JACK

Plain sailing was not on Jack Welch's route map. Quiet, contented progress was not Jack Welch's plan. He announced himself loudly rather than settling into the comfortable chair. GE was shaken and then shaken again.

And this—lest it be forgotten—was what previous incumbent Reg Jones intended to happen. "When CEO Reginald Jones and the GE board of directors selected Jack Welch, they knowingly unleashed a prophet/crusader whose management perspective was a far cry from the analytical, administrative focus that dominated GE at that point in time," wrote Al Vicere and Robert Fulmer. "Welch brought a renewed sense of purpose to the company, one that helped GE regain its balance between the forces for innovative creativity and the forces for adaptive control."[14]

During the 1980s, Welch put his dynamic mark on GE and on corporate America. GE's businesses were overhauled. Some were cast out and hundreds of new businesses were acquired. In 1984 *Fortune* called Welch the "toughest boss in America." GE's workforce bore the brunt of Welch's quest for competitiveness. GE virtually invented downsizing. Nearly 200,000 GE employees left the company. Over $6 billion was saved.

Welch was reincarnated, in the media at least, as *Neutron Jack*. He was the man who swept people away while leaving the buildings intact. Not surprisingly, he wasn't the most popular man in GE or the wider corporate world. For a while it seemed as though Welch could be bracketed alongside Al Dunlap as public enemy number one. Within GE there were grave concerns about what was happening. It was, Welch coolly reflected, part of the job, not a nice part but one that was necessary. "I didn't start with a morale problem. I created it!" he told Richard

Pascale with typical forceful candor. "The leader who tries to move a large organization counter to what his followers perceive to be necessary has a very difficult time. I had never had to do this before. I had always had the luxury of building a business and being the cheerleader. But it was clear that we had to reposition ourselves and put our chips on those businesses that could survive on a global scale."[15]

STAGE TWO: WORK-OUT

Stage one of life under Jack Welch was a brutal introduction to the new realities of business. Perhaps Welch was too brutal. But, there is no denying that by the end of the 1980s GE was a leaner and fitter organization. Any complacency that may have existed had been eradicated. In retrospect, Welch's greatest decision may have been to go in with all guns blazing. Dramatic, though relatively short-lived change, was preferable to incremental change. "Shun the incremental and go for the leap" is Welch's advice.[16] No half measures. It is an approach that Tom Peters has lauded in characteristically ebullient fashion: "Will Welch pull it off? I bet he does. Whether it's blowing the joint up ('Neutron Jack' of the early 1980s) or preaching empowerment ('Work-out Jack' of the early 1990s) . . . the bloke doesn't understand halfway measures. Jack Welch: Charter Member of the Lunatic fringe. Hooray!"[17]

Having proved that he could tear the company apart, Welch had to move on to stage two: rebuilding a company fit for the 21st century. The hardware had been taken care of. Now came the software.

Central to this was the concept of Work-out, which was launched in 1989. This came about, it is reputed, after a chance question was asked by Professor Kirby Warren of Columbia University. Warren asked Welch: "Now that you have gotten so many people out of the organization, when are you going to get some of the work out?"[18] At this stage 100,000 people had left GE. Welch liked the idea of getting the work out. The idea turned into a reality. With typical gusto, Welch brought in 20 or so business school professors and consultants to help turn the emergent concept into reality. Welch has called Work-out, "a relentless, endless company-wide search for a better way to do everything we do."[19]

Work-Out was a communication tool that offered GE employees a dramatic opportunity to change their working lives. "The idea was to hold a three-day, informal town meeting with 40 to 100 employees from all ranks of GE. The boss kicked things off by reviewing the business and laying out the agenda, then he or she left. The employees broke into groups, and aided by a facilitator, attacked separate parts of the problem," explains Janet Lowe in *Jack Welch Speaks*. "At the end, the boss returned to hear the proposed solutions. The boss had only three options: The idea could be accepted on the spot; rejected on the spot; or more information could be requested. If the boss asked for more information, he had to name a team and set a deadline for making a decision."[20]

Work-Out was astonishingly successful. It helped begin the process of rebuilding the bonds of trust between GE employees and management. It gave employees a channel through which they could talk about what concerned them at work and then actually change the way things were done. It broke down barriers. The gales of destruction were past. Creativity was in the air.

STAGE THREE: SIX SIGMA

Welch the destroyer became Welch the empowerer. Work-Out was part of a systematic opening up of GE. Walls between departments and functions came tumbling down. Middle management layers had been stripped away in the 1980s. With Work-Out, Welch was enabling and encouraging GE people to talk to each other, work together and share information and experiences. At first surprised, they soon reveled in the opportunity.

"In the early 1990s, after we had finished defining ourselves as a company of boundaryless people with a thirst for learning and a compulsion to share, it became unthinkable for any of us to tolerate—much less hire or promote—the tyrant, the turf defender, the autocrat, the big shot. They were simply yesterday," noted GE's 1997 Annual Report.

The next stage in Welch's revolution was the introduction of a wide-ranging quality program. Entitled Six Sigma, it was launched at the end of 1995. "Six Sigma has spread like wildfire across the company, and it is transforming everything we do," the company reported two years later.[21]

Six Sigma basically spread the responsibility for quality. Instead of being a production issue, quality was recast as an issue for every single person in the company. "We blew up the old quality organization, because they were off to the side. Now, it's the job of the leader, the job of the manager, the job of the employee—everyone's job is quality," said Welch.[22]

The three stages of development—destruction, creation and quality—have reshaped GE. The high-performing giant remains a high-performing giant, but one that is lean and nimble. The figures stack up nicely.

Back in 1981 as Jack Welch began life as CEO, GE had total assets of $20 billion and revenues of $27.24 billion. Its earnings were $1.65 billion. With 440,000 employees worldwide, GE had a market value of $12 billion.

By 1997, GE's total assets had mushroomed to $272.4 billion and total revenues to $79.18 billion. Around 260,000 employees—down a staggering 180,000—produced earnings of $7.3 billion and gave the company a market value of $200 billion.

GE now operates in over 100 countries with 250 manufacturing plants in 26 countries. Its workforce totals 276,000 with 165,000 in the U.S. The company's 1997 revenues were $90.84 billion with net earnings of $8.203 billion. The company's market value (according to the 1997 Annual Report) was the highest in the world: $300 billion. As a total entity, GE was ranked fifth in the most recent Fortune 500. Nine of GE's businesses would be in Fortune's top 50 if ranked independently. GE remains a corporate giant. Now, it appears to be big in all the right places.

THE GE BUSINESS

- **Aircraft engines:** In 1996-97, GE won 70 percent of the world's large commercial jet engine orders. It is the world's largest producer of large and small jet engines for aircraft.

- **Appliances:** GE Appliances sells over 10 million appliances in 150 world markets, including refrigerators, freezers, ranges, cooktops, wall ovens, dishwashers and washing machines. Its brands include the Monogram, GE Profile, Hotpoint, RCA and private label brands.

- **Capital services:** GE Capital is the star in GE's firmament. From being a sideline it has become a high-performing diversified financial company.

- **Industrial systems:** Circuit breakers, switches, transformers, switchgear, meters, etc.

- **Information services:** Business-to-business electronic commerce solutions. GE manages the world's largest electronic trading community with more than 40,000 trading partners.

- **Lighting:** From halogen lamps to outdoor lighting, GE supplies lighting for consumer, commercial and industrial markets.
- **Medical systems:** Medical diagnostic imaging technology including x-ray equipment.
- **Broadcasting:** GE owns the U.S. television network NBC which owns, among other assets, the U.S. rights to the Olympics until 2008. Various other operations include CNBC and MSNBC.
- **Plastics:** Engineered plastics for a variety of industries including building and computing.
- **Power systems:** The design, manufacture and service of gas, steam and hydroelectric turbines and generators and, controversially, nuclear fuels and services.
- **Transportation systems:** Locomotives and similar products. GE makes more than half of the diesel freight locomotives in North America.

GE NUMBER CRUNCHING[23]

Workforce:	276,000 (165,000 in the U.S.)
Revenues:	$90.84 billion
Net earnings:	$8.203 billion
Market value:	$300 billion
Value of exports from U.S.:	$11.3 billion
International revenues:	$38.5 billion (42 percent)
New plant and equipment expenditure:	$2.2 billion
R&D expenditure:	$1.9 billion
Total assets:	$304 billion

WELCH THE MANAGEMENT SUPERHERO

The plaudits roll in. From Neutron Jack to Six Sigma, Jack Welch has attracted more media coverage than most CEOs ever dream of. Most of it has been good. "If leadership is an art, then surely Welch has proved himself a master painter," said *BusinessWeek*. The magazine has also noted that Welch is "the gold standard against which other CEOs are measured."[24]

Yet Welch remains a character with whom many—not only at GE—feel an affinity. His humble roots, plain talking and huge success make an alluring combination. He appears ordinary. Everyone calls him Jack. There is still a slight stutter when he speaks. "With his squat, muscular, five-foot, eight-inch frame, pasty complexion, and Boston accent, the 62-year old balding man looks and sounds more like the guy behind the wheel of a bus on Beacon Hill," noted one *BusinessWeek* article.[25]

All in all it has been quite a turnaround. Personally, Welch has moved from arch destroyer, corporate enemy number one, to potent creator. "The most acclaimed SOB of the last decade is the most acclaimed CEO of this one," announced *Industry Week* in 1994.[26] The corporate demon king of the 1980s has been transformed into the role model for twenty-first-century management. "The two greatest corporate leaders of this century are Alfred Sloan of General Motors and Jack Welch of GE. And Welch would be the

"The most acclaimed SOB of the last decade is the most acclaimed CEO of this one."

greater of the two because he set a new, contemporary paradigm for the corporation that is the model for the twenty-first-century," says the University of Michigan's Noel Tichy, a longtime observer of the Welch managerial style.[27]

GE itself has experienced a turnaround. The company wasn't exactly ailing in the first place, but equally, it wasn't going anywhere fast. Under Welch, GE has moved from steady juggernaut to the fast-expanding, forever accelerating corporate model for the next century.

Beneath this transformation lies a coherent approach to and philosophy of management and business: business the Jack Welch way. I have identified ten essential ingredients of Welch's managerial style:

1. **Invest in people.** People matter. Talking to them and meeting them takes up a serious chunk of Jack Welch's time. So, too, does developing people for the future. He talks, pontificates, cajoles and educates. But, most of all, he connects.

2. **Dominate your market . . . or get out.** The choice is simple and is repeatedly laid out by Jack Welch. He has no time for companies that are fourth or fifth in their market. He wants to be first or a close second. Gain market leadership and take the market by the scruff of the neck and lead it forward. If you can't get to the front, sell the business and look elsewhere.

3. **Never sit still.** Jack Welch is restless. Despite heart surgery, he never stops. He has inculcated GE with the same sort of restless energy. The company won't stay still or rest on its laurels. GE changes and then changes again. It is always nearer its goals by never staying in one place.

4. **Think service.** Pre-Welch, GE was a manufacturer, a good old-fashioned champion of the smokestacks. Welch introduced it to service. Now GE is a service company that also manufactures. It is a finance company and an information company as well as a maker of appliances. Quality and service link its activities.

5. **Forget the past; love the future.** For a company with such a great history, GE under Welch has become preoccupied with the future. It embraces the new—whether it be IT or the Internet. Welch envisions the future. He speaks enthusiastically about the future. And GE creates the future.

6. **Learn and lead.** The new model leader is not a corporate dictator. The leader is committed to learning, deciding and moving forward. Wrong decisions present their own opportunities. Learning from failure is more important than wallowing in success.

7. **No bull.** Jack Welch communicates. He is straight. Whether he is talking to workers in a GE factory, managers on a training program or industry analysts, he speaks with passionate clarity. He tells it as it is.

8. **Kill bureaucracy.** Dismayed by the time-wasting of bureaucracy and hierarchy, Jack Welch nearly left GE after his first year. He was talked into staying, but the bugbear remained. Since taking over at the top, Welch has eradicated bureaucracy with a vengance.

9. **Stick around.** The corporate person is supposedly dead. But Jack Welch has done all right sticking with a single employer. How has he managed to learn and develop in a single organization?

10. **Manage the corner store.** Jack Welch manages GE as if it were a corner store. The same things matter: quality and service; cash flow; keeping abreast of what sells, what part of the business is doing well; people. The fact that you are selling nuclear power plants and not candy bars is immaterial.

NOTES

1 Lowe, Janet, *Jack Welch Speaks*, John Wiley, New York, 1998.

2 Peters, Tom, *Thriving on Chaos*, Alfred A Knopf, New York, 1987.

3 Mintzberg, Henry.

4 Swoboda, Frank, "Jack Welch and the boundaryless company," *Washington Post*, February 27, 1994.

5 "Passing the torch," *Monogram*, January–February 1981.

6 Tichy, Noel and Sherman, Stratford, *Control Your Own Destiny or Someone Else Will*, Doubleday Currency, New York, 1993.

7 De Geus, Arie, *The Living Company*, Harvard Business School Press, Boston, 1997.

8 Pascale, Richard, *Managing on the Edge*, Simon & Schuster, New York, 1990.

9 Porras, Jerry and Collins, James, *Built to Last*, Century, New York, 1997.

10 Elfun Society History, www.elfun.org

11 Hambrick, D, and Fukotoni, GDS, "The seasons of a CEO's tenure," *Academy of Management Review*, Vol 16, No. 4, 1991.

12 Pascale, Richard, *Managing on the Edge*, Simon & Schuster, New York, 1990.

13 Pascale, Richard, *Managing on the Edge*, Simon & Schuster, New York, 1990.

14 Vicere, Albert and Fulmer, Robert, *Leadership By Design*, Harvard Business School Press, Boston, 1998.

15 Pascale, Richard, *Managing on the Edge*, Simon & Schuster, New York, 1990.

16 Welch, Jack, "Shun the incremental and go for the leap," *Financier*, July 1984.

17 Peters, Tom, *The Circle of Innovation*, Knopf, New York, 1997.

18 Vicere, Albert and Fulmer, Robert, *Leadership by Design*, Harvard Business School Press, Boston, 1998.

19 General Electric Annual General Meeting, 1990.

20 Lowe, Janet, *Jack Welch Speaks*, John Wiley, New York, 1998.

21 Byrne, John, "How Jack Welch runs GE," *Business Week*, 8 June 1998.

22 Lowe, Janet, *Jack Welch Speaks*, John Wiley, New York, 1998.

23 General Electric Annual Report, 1997.

24 Smart, Tim, "Jack Welch's encore," *Business Week*, October 28, 1996.

25 Byrne, John, "How Jack Welch runs GE," *Business Week*, June 8, 1998.

26 Day, Charles R. Jr and LaBarre, Polly, "GE: Just your average everyday $60 billion family grocery store," *Industry Week*, May 2, 1994.

27 Byrne, John, "How Jack Welch runs GE," *Business Week*, June 8, 1998.

Invest in People

Your most precious possession is not your financial assets. Your most precious possession is the people you have working there, and what they carry around in their heads, and their ability to work together.

ROBERT REICH[1]

PEOPLE POWER

How many CEOs have you heard pronounce that people are their company's most important assets? Plenty. How many mean it? How many actually convert that corporate truism into practice day in and day out? Not many.

"By the time people become CEOs they are preoccupied with survival and money. They respond to capital markets, stockholders, etc. Even if they try or want to be people-oriented, a financial crisis will always get their attention," says MIT's Ed Schein.[2] Jack Welch appears to be an exception. People are the bread and butter of his managerial style. People matter—or are made to feel as though they matter. Says Welch: "We are betting everything on our people—empowering them, giving them resources, and getting out of their way."[3]

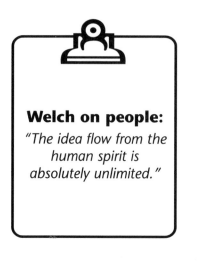

Welch on people:

"The idea flow from the human spirit is absolutely unlimited."

Welch invests in people first by simply spending time with them. Jack Welch calculates that he spends around half of his time with GE people, getting to know them, talking to them about their problems and, yes, no doubt berating them if performances are down. It has been calculated that he knows around 1000 people by name, with a good idea of their job responsibilities.

He does so because he is an optimist about human potential. "The idea flow from the human spirit is absolutely unlimited. All you have to do is tap into that well. I don't like to use the word efficiency. It's creativity. It's a belief that every person counts," he says.[4]

This is not touchy-feely stuff. Jack Welch wants the best people. He wants to recruit them and retain them because it is good for his business. "The reality is, we simply cannot afford to field anything but teams of A players," he says. "What is an A? At the leadership level, an A is a man or woman with a vision and the ability to articulate that vision to the team, so vividly and powerfully that it also becomes their vision. An A leader has enormous personal energy and, beyond that, the ability to energize others and draw out their best, usually on a global basis. An A leader had edge as well: the instinct and the courage to make the tough calls—decisively, but with fairness and absolute integrity."[5]

Clearly, Welch wants people to perform. He insists that rewards packages be geared to individual as well as corporate achievements and ensures that rewards are carefully monitored and differentiated from business to business and person to person. The message is that if you win we, all win. That's why 27,000 GE employees now have stock options.

"I want a revolution, and I want it to start at Crotonville."

It is not only that Jack Welch spends time with people; he also expresses constant commitment to developing them. Early on he promised, "I want a revolution, and I want it to start at Crotonville."[6] Crotonville is GE's legendary Management Development Institute, established in 1956. Welch is a regular visitor and teacher at the center. It is estimated that in 250 sessions he has personally talked to some 15,000 of the company's executives.

The message from Crotonville is that developing people is too important a task to be delegated to business schools or training companies. Crotonville says that its mission "is to leverage GE's global competitiveness as an instrument of cultural change, by improving business acumen, leadership abilities and organization effectiveness of GE professionals." Noel Tichy (now of the University of Michigan and an ex-Crotonville director) has called Crotonville "a staging ground for a corporate revolution."[7]

Putting such bold statements to one side, there is little doubt that Crotonville has given GE a clear headstart over most of its rivals. Few other companies have managed to adapt the best managerial ideas to their particular circumstances with such frequency over such an extended period of time. From

Management By Objectives in the 1950s to Six Sigma in the 1990s, GE has effectively cherrypicked management ideas. Crotonville has also helped imbue the GE culture into generations of managers. (Such is its power that in his work on corporate culture MIT's Ed Schein has made comparisons between the activities of Crotonville and similar institutions and wartime brainwashing. To some, this could be a complement.)

Only now is the Crotonville model becoming fashionable. The trend towards do-it-yourself management development is strongest in the United States where over 1000 corporate colleges are now operating. They now come in all shapes and sizes, and cover virtually every industry. The Ohio automotive-parts manufacturer, Dana Corporation, has Dana University; Ford has a Heavy Truck University in Detroit; Intel runs a university in Santa Clara; Sun Microsystems has Sun U; and Apple has its own university in Cupertino, California.

The growth in corporate universities can largely be attributed to two ideas. First, critics of traditional business schools have repeatedly accused them of being too far from the pulse of the business world. It is a widely perceived weakness that corporate universities are keen to capitalize on. B-schools can't get Jack Welch to deliver a lecture on leadership.

The second impetus behind the growth of corporate universities is the realization that developing people is the key to future survival, something that is too important to be delegated to an external organization. American research found that companies with their own universities spent 2.5 percent of payroll on learning—double the U.S. national average. GE is not in the habit of delegating something so important to an outside organization.

Clearly, Crotonville, with its teachers and resources, is a huge investment. Corporate universities are not for the fainthearted. They are highly expensive. Research in the U.S. by Jeanne Meister calculated that the average operating budget for a corporate university was $12.4 million (though 60 per cent reported budgets of $5 million or less). Typically, National Semiconductor University, opened in 1994, occupies 22,000 square foot premises with nine classrooms and room for 430 students. Such facilities—as business schools have been pointing out for years—are costly. Running Intel University cost the company $150 million in 1996. GE's Crotonville is an investment in people, a big investment.

PLAN FOR THE FUTURE

Welch not only connects with and develops people but he also invests in the company's future. He is concerned with who becomes the next CEO. He wants to exercise influence over the next cadre of management. He wants the GE way to exist long after his retirement. In many ways, Welch is passing on the baton. Reg Jones, his predecessor, did much the same, assiduously preparing Welch for his future role.

Such succession planning makes good sense. It is often mentioned as sound management practice. It is amazing, therefore, that there are so few signs of it actually being practiced successfully. The reasons for this are undoubtedly complex, but there is the suspicion that succession planning is a rarity because senior managers don't really care what happens when they go; are too wrapped up in their daily activities to think

"Effective leaders recognize that the ultimate test of leadership is sustained success, which demands the constant cultivation of future leaders."

ahead; or like to think of themselves as executive immortals.

However, looking to the future and creating the next generation of executives is also a central role of leadership. Leaving a power vacuum is hardly effective leadership. "Effective leaders recognize that the ultimate test of leadership is sustained success, which demands the constant cultivation of future leaders," says Noel Tichy.[8] Leaders must therefore invest in developing the leaders of tomorrow and they must communicate directly with those who will follow in their footsteps.

Tichy cites a number of examples. Larry Bossidy, CEO of AlliedSignal (and formerly with GE), put all the company's 86,000 employees through a development program and managed to speak to 15,000 of them during his first year in the job.[9] Along the way, Bossidy also increased the market value of the company by 400 percent in six years. Other exemplars are the usual suspects, including Andy Grove of Intel, Welch, and Lew Platt of Hewlett-Packard.

Tichy believes that being able to pass on leadership skills to others requires three things. First, a "teachable point of view"—"You must be able to talk clearly and convincingly about who you are, why you exist and how you operate." Second, the leader requires a story. "Dramatic storytelling is the way people learn from one another," Tichy writes, suggesting that this explains why Bill Gates and the like feel the need to write books.

The third element in passing on the torch of leadership is teaching methodology. "To be a great teacher you have to be a great learner." The great corporate leaders are hungry to know more and do not regard their knowledge as static or comprehensive.

Welch passes all three tests with ease. He teaches at Crotonville and professes to enjoy it. He connects with people because he is keen to find out more about them and their problems. Finally, as we shall see, learning is one of the cornerstones of his leadership style.

INVEST IN PEOPLE

♦ **Communicate constantly with everyone.** *The leader does not exercise leadership in a vacuum but must enable others to fulfil their potential through communicating inside and outside the organization. Talk and then talk some more.*

♦ **Avoid isolation:** *"Leadership is about a commitment to people," says British Airways chairman Sir Colin Marshall, before issuing the warning, "People at the top of the organizational hierarchy must have access to people in the workplace. If they don't they quickly become cut off."[10] Communication is a lifeline. The leader who fails to communicate quickly becomes cut off, a prisoner in the executive suite.*

The great leaders appear to avoid becoming isolated with relative and intuitive, ease. Mere mortals have to guard constantly against becoming out of touch.

This is the antithesis of the traditional notion of the "great man" school of leadership in which the leader is, by necessity, an isolated and indomitable figure. Today's leaders are skeptical of retaining an objective distance, believing that objectivity can lead to aloofness. Instead, they place emphasis on their humanity and accessibility. Leaders are also human and, of course, along with this comes the realization that they are fallible.

♦ **Develop people's skills for today and tomorrow.** *Talent is the scarcest of resources. Research by McKinsey & Co. covering nearly 6000 managers in 77 companies concluded that the hunt to recruit and retain talented people has never been more intense. McKinsey's Ed Michaels is terse: "All that matters is talent. Talent wins."[11] As GE has long realized, developing talent is the surest route to competitive advantage. Unlike strategies, it cannot be easily emulated. The problem is worsened in the U.S. at least by demographics. In 15 years the numbers of 35- to 45-year-olds will be down 15 percent.*

Attracting the best people revolves around four baits. People want to join companies that are perceived as winners; those that offer high risks with high salaries; those perceived as industry- or world-changing; or, finally, those that complement their lifestyles. Companies ignore such aspirations at their peril.

♦ **Manage succession.** *Any leader must not only provide an active lead in the present, but must plan for the future leadership of the organization. This is something that some of the great leaders—from Churchill to Margaret Thatcher—have overlooked. In doing so, they run the risk of having their legacy tarnished.*

Perhaps the most forceful explanation of the importance of succession planning is given by British executive Sir Adrian Cadbury. To him, the leader who neglects those around him or her is failing to exercise leadership. "True leaders encourage their followers to develop their talents and to grow in stature.

> They build their successors, so that, in time, their leadership will no longer be needed," says Cadbury. "False leaders take away from their followers the ability to decide for themselves; they hold them in thrall and diminish them as people. The tests in essence are simple ones, good leaders grow people, bad leaders stunt them; good leaders serve their followers, bad leaders enslave them."

NOTES

1 Crainer, Stuart, *The Ultimate Book of Business Quotations*, Capstone, Oxford, 1997.

2 Author interview.

3 Stewart, Thomas, "GE keeps those ideas coming," *Fortune*, August 12, 1991.

4 Byrne, John, "How Jack Welch runs GE," *Business Week*, June 8, 1998.

5 General Electric Annual Report, 1997.

6 Tichy, Noel and Sherman, Stratford, *Control Your Destiny or Someone Else Will*, Doubleday Currency, New York, 1993.

7 Tichy, Noel and Sherman, Stratford, *Control Your Destiny or Someone Else Will*, Doubleday Currency, New York, 1993.

8 Tichy, Noel, "The mark of a winner," *Leader to Leader*, Fall 1997.

9 Bossidy was helpful to GE in introducing its Six Sigma quality initiative; AlliedSignal had already done so.

10 Author interview.

11 Fishman, Charles, "The war for talent," *Fast Company*, Issue 16, August/September 1998.

Dominate Your Market ... or Get Out

Once you get into number one or number two businesses and you've got scale like we have, the chances of it all going wrong are minimal. A global recession in all businesses could slow us down. But we'd be less slowed down than 99.9 percent of the institutions in the world.

JACK WELCH[1]

MARKET SHARE MAGIC

Market share first reached a mass audience in the 1960s. This was partly thanks to the Growth/Share Matrix developed by Boston Consulting Group and its founder Bruce Henderson. The Matrix measures market growth and relative market share for all the businesses in a particular industry. The hypothesis of the framework is that companies with higher market share and growth are more profitable. The further to the left a business is on the BCG Matrix, the stronger a company should be.

BCG then superimposed on the matrix a theory of cash management that included a hierarchy of uses of cash, numbered from 1 to 4 in their order of priority. Richard Koch explained them in his *Financial Times Guide to Strategy*:[2]

1. The most effective use of cash is to defend cash cows. They should not need to use cash very often,

but if investment in a new factory or technology is required, it should be made without question.

2. The next call on cash should normally be stars. These will need a great deal of investment to hold (or gain) relative market share.

3. The trouble potentially begins with BCG's third priority, to take money from cash cows and invest in question-marks.

4. The lowest priority is investment in dogs, which BCG said should be minimal or even negative, if they were run for cash.

As a measure of corporate success market share has slipped out of fashion. It is now commonly regarded as a useful but not crucial measure of corporate performance. Jack Welch, however, remains a fan. He has eyes only for stars and cash cows.

It appears somewhat strange that Welch has so unequivocally placed his faith in simple measurement of market share as a measure of how well a business is performing.

Welch has been criticized for his faith in market share. For example, in his 1992 book *Liberation Management*, Tom Peters found himself in (rare) agreement with Harvard Business School's competitiveness guru, Michael Porter: "Michael Porter has often chided CEO Jack Welch for insisting that all GE units rank no. 1, no. 2 or no. 3 in their industries. I think Porter's exactly right, if you use (as Welch apparently does) an overall measure of market share, e.g. 'share of the global appliance market,' 'share of the global computer market.' Focusing on overall share pushes you automatically toward schemes that will kill you in the long run. You will emphasise commodity (high sales) approaches and browbeat customers into hanging in with your ageing technologies."[3]

So why has Jack Welch resurrected market share? The reasons are simple:

First, market share is an easily understood rallying point. Everyone in the business, no matter what they do or where they do it, can understand what market share means.

Second, market share gives businesses a clear criteria for success or failure. They know where they stand. The seemingly arbitrary nature of acquisitions and divestments is eliminated.

Third, market share is not an overriding philosophy. It is not an obsession, just a convenient rationale. Indeed, as we shall see, Welch has been lauded by leading strategic thinkers for using market share and then moving on.

A fourth reason is given by Andrew Campbell, Michael Goold and Marcus Alexander in their book, *Corporate-Level Strategy*: "GE tends to be in businesses in which market share matters and is important for competitive success. Thus an emphasis on building number one or two positions in the relevant markets creates value. Conversely, GE is less at home in, and has tended to avoid, businesses where market leadership provides few advantages, or where rapid swings in market tastes, or in product or process technologies, can undermine the advantages of an established leader."[4]

"GE tends to be in businesses in which market share matters and is important for competitive success."

MARKET SHARE AND BEYOND

Adrian Slywotsky, David Morrison and James Quella of Mercer Management Consulting have proclaimed that "Market share is dead."[5] They argue that success is dependent on three "capabilities": "Strategic Anticipation, identifying future value creation opportunities; Business Design, designing the enterprise so that it is able to seize those opportunities; value growth realization, moving rapidly and successfully from the old Business Design to the new one."

Slywotzky, Morrison and Quella provide another angle on Welch's management of GE. They believe his success demonstrates Strategic Anticipation, Business Design and value growth realization. Welch initially identified dominant market share as the source of strength, the "profit zone." Market share was proclaimed from the rooftops. Then he anticipated changes in GE's markets. "While good products would continue to be essential to building good customer relationships, the new profit zone would be solutions, services and outsourcing," write the consulting team. Consequently, Welch "thought beyond the product to the entire economic equation of the customer's use of the product."

GE reinvented itself as a manufacturer with service excellence—witness the explosive growth of GE Capital Services (by 1995 equivalent in size to the third biggest U.S. bank). GE went beyond mere product excellence to embrace services quality through its Six Sigma program. It looked to the future, reinvented itself and, as a result, continued to grow shareholder value.

To achieve such a transformation, say Slywotsky, Morrison and Quella, requires four crucial changes in perception: "From inside-out to outside-in; from revenue to profit; from product and technology to Business Design; from market share to value share." For GE, value has become the new rallying cry, but market share remains an important measure.

DOMINATE YOUR MARKET ... OR GET OUT

+ ***Identify clear measures for success.*** *What actually constitutes success can easily become confused. Is it sales or profits or shareholder return or return on capital invested? The answer is that it is all these things and more. Each different constituency is interested in different measures. Welch's use of market share as a measure is not a definitive statement on the matter, but it clarifies what the starting point is.*

+ ***Provide a rallying point and make sure people know what it is.*** *Market share is not the be-all and end-all of GE's performance. But it is easily understood by everyone. Jack Welch spends a lot of time banging home the message that businesses need to be number one or two in their markets. It provides focus.*

+ ***Be decisive.*** *Market share gives a clear measurement. Measurements need to be acted upon rather than collected* ad infinitum. *Performance data has to lead to action. If companies slip up, they will be sold off. Clearly established criteria enable Welch to be decisive. He can say: "I told you what the performance standards are and you didn't meet them." End of story. "Welch will say yes. Welch will say no. But he never says maybe. A lot of CEOs do, and decisions lay there like three-legged horses that no one wants to shoot," Boston Consulting Group consultant George Stalk has observed.*[6]

NOTES

1   Jackson, Tony and Gowers, Andrew, "Big enough to make mistakes," *Financial Times*, December 21, 1995.

2   Koch, Richard, *Financial Times Guide to Strategy*, F. T. Pitman, London, 1995.

3   Peters, Tom, *Liberation Management*, Alfred A. Knopf, New York, 1992.

4   Campbell, Andrew, Goold, Michael and Alexander, Marcus, *Corporate-Level Strategy*, John Wiley, New York, 1994.

5   Slywotzky, Adrian J., Morrison, David J. and Quella, James A., "Achieving sustained shareholder value growth," *Mercer Management Journal*, No. 10, 1998.

6   Byrne, John, "How Jack Welch runs GE," *Business Week*, June 8, 1998.

Never Sit Still

Jack Welch, of uppity $60-billion General Electric, is neither consistent nor predictable. Change everything, then change it again—that's his trademark.

TOM PETERS[1]

WORKING SMART

Change yourself and change your organization—
constantly. These are the twin challenges of our
corporate times. Executives must change themselves. They must develop new skills to make themselves more employable and to keep up with the heady pace of development.

Corporations must also change. The static organization is on its way to the corporate graveyard.

Jack Welch has proved himself a master of both personal and corporate change. Welch never sits still and has created an organization that likewise does not.

"Mr. Welch can spend a day visiting a factory, jump on a plane, catch a few hours' sleep, and start all over again; in between, he might stop in Sun Alley, Idaho, and as he puts it, 'ski like crazy for five days,'" noted an article in the *Wall Street Journal*.[2]

Leaders are energetic. They have to be. Margaret Thatcher slept four hours a night and rose to pore over yet more government papers. IBM's Lou Gerstner is renowned for his energy (and sleep) levels. Top executives travel constantly and yet still emerge from the arrivals lounge looking fresh, armed with a report they've just written somewhere over the ocean. David Campbell of the Center for Creative Leadership finds over and over that effective leaders and high energy go hand in hand on his Leadership Inventory.

Energy is a prerequisite for the top job. The mistake is to think that Welch's secret is quantity rather than quality. Maximizing energy is much more than running fast or working harder. Anyone can work 16 hours a day. The world is full of hardworking executives who have mortgaged their future health and family lives against their current working days. But how you spend your time and how you enthuse others is more important. Quality is vital; quantity is no longer a competitive advantage. In fact, executives who pin their faith simply on working harder are taking a route to burnout and disenchantment.

The truth is that maximizing effectiveness is more important than maximizing working hours. Research by Phil Hodgson of Ashridge Management College estimated that conventional managers probably operate at just 40 percent of their true ability. They spend 10 percent of their time being really effective by doing what is important and 30 percent of their time gaining credibility in order to be really effective for that other 10 percent. The rest of the time they spend doing things that are not important or don't produce the outcome they want.[3] Do the important things more often and more intensively and you will be working smart.

Working smart, Jack Welch style, has a number of features:

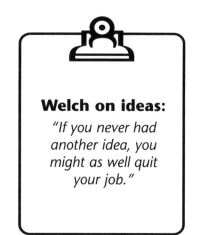

- **Every day is different. Every day is a challenge.** "Who runs out of ideas?" asks Welch. "If you never had another idea, you might as well quit your job. Every day we wake up, there's another basket of opportunities. When you're a $70 billion company, you're doing so many things wrong that the amount available for improvement is literally infinite. Our improvements are getting greater with time, not diminishing."[4] Such relentless positivism insists that things can be sorted out, improved, solved. And, it works.

- **Peel away the layers. Reverse engineer.** Leaders have to dig deep and deeper and deeper still. They must peel away the layers. Executives must look for problems to solve. And then there is another problem, and another. Welch is an engineer by training and the urge to ask questions and figure out what is really happening has never left him.

- **Love your job.** It helps, of course, if you actually regard what you do as important. The job must matter. Why else is Jack Welch running GE after a triple bypass or Michael Eisner still at Disney after his heart attack? For such leaders, financial motivation is limited. Billionaires tend not to worry quite so much about their next paycheck. They are not angelic figures who regard financial rewards as unimportant. They expect to be well rewarded, but look beyond the narrow motivation of money alone.

♦ **Get a life.** "I spend enough hours to get the job done," Welch once said.[5] He is not one of those macho execs who constantly refers to working 23 hours a day and sleeping for five nanoseconds. (Of course, the fact that he does not say it repeatedly does not mean that he doesn't work long hours. It's just not a big deal.) Jack Welch, strange as it may seem, has a life outside GE. It is a fairly ordinary life. For such a powerful and wealthy man it is a very quiet life. He lives opposite a golf club to ensure that the first tee is never far away. He doesn't fill his few spare hours with non-executive directorships or other peripheral stuff. He enjoys getting his handicap down and recharging. Smart.

LEARN AND CHANGE[6]

Not only has Jack Welch worked smart: He has developed smart. His career has missed the stagnancy of middle age. He has kept on learning, adding to his formidable battery of skills. He has changed and then changed some more. In doing so he has defied a commonplace pattern.

Look at how our careers develop. In the first place, we watch the corporate video or attend an induction program to know the basics of what is expected of us: the corporate values and behavior. Then we go up through the first level of performance and are taught the essential things to survive and prosper in that business. Perhaps it is selling, perhaps it is computing, perhaps it is accounting. Whatever it is we are given the basic rules: Master marketing and you will progress. Good financiers get to the top here.

Then, if we are very good, we move into a second layer where we can start to adapt some of the things we have been taught to local circumstances. But if we come up against something we really don't know, our best way of dealing with it is to go and ask someone who does know to help us enhance our knowledge.

During this process, the developing executive is highly conscious of his or her vulnerability. As we have seen, learning involves taking a risk and taking risks makes us vulnerable. People are afraid to make themselves more vulnerable, to expose themselves to potential loss of face, loss of opportunity or simply loss.

As a result, the executives develop what has been accurately labeled as a myth of mastery. By steering clear of trouble spots, situations that make them vulnerable, executives begin to believe that they are invincible. In their own minds they are, in Tom Wolfe's phrase, "Masters of the Universe."

In turn, this provides a formula for executive progression. The people who reach the top are high performers who don't make mistakes. They get it right, but sacrifice things to get it right. They are often better at a particular skill than the people who work for them. They are perfectionists with high IQs who don't tolerate dips in performance. They are also superstitious—believing that if they do what they've always done, things will come out right.

As an adjunct to the myth of mastery, executives are often promoted because they are good technically, not because they are good with people. Technical skills—whether they are in marketing, finance or technology—are measurable and there for all to see. Executives master the business equivalent of the slam dunk and keep doing it. Contrast this with managing people, which despite the best efforts of academics remains steadfastly immeasurable. If it can't be measured it tends to be neglected or overlooked. For CEOs, managing people is the source of their greatest frustration and often their greatest area of ignorance. (Not so, as we have seen, for Jack Welch, a member of that most socially dysfunctional group: one-company engineers.)

What happens then is that executives get found out. After they are promoted it becomes clear that they are ill-prepared for their new jobs. Their flaws are there for all to see. They may be insensitive or aloof, but as these characteristics have never been truly tested at the lower level they never became apparent till now, when it is probably too late to do very much about them.

Given the standard career progression it is little wonder that senior executives are highly proficient until it comes to dealing with people. Think of how the standard executive career unfolds. There are three leaps in the development of most people's careers. Their first supervisory experience teaches them that it's more than just the technical aspects of the job—people are a problem.

Then, at mid-levels in most people's careers, they are faced with the first leadership paradox. Suddenly, technical mastery of a given area isn't enough because the people who work for you will know more about a particular area than you. Learning to direct and motivate people who often do not want you to be their leader becomes a necessary skill. You also need to learn to be a creative problem solver, sorting the strategic from the tactical and the urgent from the non-urgent.

The toughest transition is to become a generalist, a general manager. Harvard's John Kotter, in *The General Managers*, suggests that it takes 20 years to become one.[7] (Jack Welch was right on time.) At this level, you are supposed to be strategic *and* able to deal with ambiguity. Here there are no right or wrong answers but only good, better and best answers. It is also at this level that one has the potential to understand higher-order people skills like: I can't do this job well by myself, I need the team to get it done.[8] So the skills that propel executives up the ladder are not the leadership skills and perspectives needed for making it to the top. Higher-order people skills, strategic skills and the skills necessary to deal with uncertainty are needed.

The top job involves having the humility to understand that you do not know it all. It also involves keen awareness of ambiguity, something managers are often ill-equipped to deal with. Jack Welch has the humility to admit that he does not know and to learn some more. He is also keenly aware that the uncertainty of organizational life means that simple answers may be elusive. It is often not a case of either/or but of either/and.

Says Welch: "Effective leadership involves the acceptance and management of paradox. For example, we must function collectively as one company and individually as many businesses at the same time."[9]

Welch on managing for the long term:

"You can't grow long-term if you can't eat short-term. Anybody can manage short. Anybody can manage long. Balancing those two things is what management is."

Elsewhere Welch has referred to management as a balancing act between the present and the future. "You can't grow long-term if you can't eat short-term. Anybody can manage short. Anybody can manage long. Balancing those two things is what management is," says Welch.[10] Management is therefore not a matter of answers and solutions, but a precarious balancing act. You have to accept that you will fall off from time to time. The myth of mastery is nothing more than a myth.

ENERGY MOTIVATES

Welch's energy plays a crucial role in motivating others and in liberating energy in others. High performers like Welch discover energy from the mundane, from the routine. They extract ideas to generate enthusiasm. They invent different approaches and try new things. They generate energy from themselves and stimulate energy in those they work with. They attract people with energy.

The most obvious manifestation of their energy is their sheer enthusiasm. It is something they carefully cultivate and nurture, and it is highly infectious. Go to a Tom Peters seminar and even if you do not remember a single idea, you will remember that Peters is an enthusiast who can transmit his enthusiasm so

Welch on energy:
"The world will belong to passionate, driven leaders—people who not only have enormous amounts of energy but who can energize those whom they lead."

that people begin to believe in their own potential. Leaders transmit energy.

Says Welch: "The world of the 1990s and beyond will not belong to 'managers' or those who can make the numbers dance. The world will belong to passionate, driven leaders—people who not only have enormous amounts of energy but who can energize those whom they lead."[11] Energy motivates. Listless leaders lead listless organizations.

CHANGE, THEN CHANGE AGAIN

The family-run Stone Container Corporation of Chicago would appear to have little need to reinvent itself for the future. Its profitability grew fifteenfold in the 1980s, boosting annual sales to $5.5 billion. Yet speaking at the 1993 meeting of the International Strategic Management Society, the company's president and chief executive, Roger Stone, described how his company was revitalizing itself.

The keys to modern corporate learning and transformation, according to Stone, are: to become even more "customer-driven" and quality-focused; to stimulate innovation throughout the company; to measure corporate and individual performance on every possible dimension; to "manage backwards from the future, rather than short-term"; to simplify structures and processes; and, most importantly, to foster a process of "creative discontent" within the company. Stone concluded: "If you want to be content you should be a dog."[12]

Stone got it right. Complacency is the root of all corporate evil. Sit still and you die. There are the quick and the dead, as the popular saying goes.

Jack Welch's personal energy levels have set the tone for GE. He refuses to give in to the myth of complacency. So, too, does GE. It wriggles and changes in front of your eyes, moving with the times to get ahead of the times.

Crucially, GE has refused to rest on its well-endowed laurels, a temptation most organizations submit to at some time or another. Richard Pascale's *Managing on the Edge*[13] begins with the warning: "Nothing fails like success." "Great strengths are inevitably the root of weakness," argues Pascale, pausing only to point out that from the Fortune 500 of 1985, 143 had departed five years later.

Pascale contends that four factors "drive stagnation and renewal in organizations":

1. *Fit* pertains to an organization's internal consistency (unity).
2. *Split* describes a variety of techniques for breaking a bigger organization into smaller units and providing them with a stronger sense of ownership and identity (plurality).
3. *Contend* refers to a management process that harnesses (rather than suppresses) the contradictions that are inevitable by-products of organizations (duality).
4. *Transcend* alerts us to the higher order of complexity that successfully managing the renewal process entails (vitality).

To overcome inertia and survive in a turbulent climate requires a constant commitment to what Pascale labels "corporate transformation." Change, says Pascale, is a fact of business life. The trouble is we are ill-equipped to deal with it and our traditional approach to managing change is no longer applicable. "The incremental approach to change is effective when what you want is more of what you've already got. Historically, that has been sufficient because our advantages of plentiful resources, geographical isolation, and absence of serious global competition defined a league in which we competed with ourselves and everyone played by the same rules."

True transformation requires the involvement and commitment of all in the organization. The problem with programs of change does not usually lie with the programs themselves. Instead, their central limitation is that they are driven by and involve so few people. The genius of GE's Work-Out, therefore, was that it launched a program of listening and of change that involved as many people as possible. It did not come from the top. Indeed, its very structure encouraged those at the bottom to take their chances and take the lead.

According to Pascale, incorporating employees fully into the principal business challenges facing the company is the first "intervention" required if companies are to thrive. The second is to lead the organization in a way that sharpens and maintains incorporation and "constructive stress." Finally, Pascale advocates instilling mental disciplines that will make people behave differently and then helping them sustain their new behavior. In the latter element, Pascale cites the work of the United States Army, in which a strong culture allows minds and behavior to be changed through rigorous and carefully thought-through training. (If this sounds familiar think of Crotonville and its long-term impact on the way people at GE think and behave.)

In particular, Pascale has examined the work of the Army's National Training Center in California. "The Army's success stems from: every one of its soldiers having a shared and intricate understanding of what drives 'business results'; cultivating relentless discomfort with the status quo . . . and establishing a standard of uncompromising straight talk that evokes cross-hierarchical feedback and introspection," he says.[14]

The Center puts units of 3000 to 4000 people through a gruelling 14-day program involving 600 instructors, 18-hour days, simulated battles and "After Action Reviews" where, says Pascale, "hardship and insight meet." Pascale believes that what makes this intense training effective is its concentration on identifying the key tasks that drive success; the immersion of the teams in the tasks they encounter; the collection of hard data to avoid subjectivity and needless debate; the use of highly trained facilitators; and a fundamental belief in not criticizing people. Interestingly, the Center does not evaluate performance. Instead its onus is on how much each person can learn. The lessons for industry are important, says Pascale: Only immersion in an environment of learning, constant questioning and openness can create a culture geared to transformation. (The one drawback in converting the Army's methods into the corporate world is cost—"all it takes is 650,000 acres and a million dollars a day.")

In his recent work, Pascale has coined the term "agility" to describe the combination of skills and thinking required of the organizations of the future. Pascale and his coresearchers believe that there are "four indicators that tell us a great deal about how an organization is likely to perform and adapt." These are power (Do employees think they can have any influence on the course of events?); identity (To what extent do individuals identify with the organization as a whole, rather than with a narrow group?); contention (Is conflict brought out into the open and used as a learning tool?); and learning (How does the organization deal with new ideas?).[15]

The trouble is that these four elements, under normal circumstances, tend to coagulate and the organization eventually stagnates. Pascale says that this can only be avoided if an organization pursues seven disciplines of agility, which range from the self-explanatory "accountability in action" to the more elusive and painful "course of relentless discomfort."

The course of relentless discomfort is the one chosen by Jack Welch. There is no point in settling safely down in your comfort zone. You have to get out there and shake things up, find out more, uncover and discover. You don't have to join the Army but you can't do it from a desk.

NEVER SIT STILL

♦ *Get fit. Couch potatoes struggle to keep up. Today's corporate chieftains have constitutions as formidable as their profits.*

♦ *Pick people with energy. GE's only worry is finding people who can keep up with Welch.*

♦ *Know your job. Ask CEOs what their job is and you usually get a reply about strategy and vision. Often, you realize, they have very little idea what their jobs*

---

are. It is too general. There is too much of it to actually distill it down to a couple of lines. The reality in such cases is often that CEOs spend so much time putting out fires that they have very little idea what their jobs should be. Dealing with the day's disasters does not have a noble ring to it.

Now, try asking Jack Welch what his job is. He is falling over himself to tell you.

"My job is to find great ideas, exaggerate them, and spread them like hell around the business with the speed of light," he told Industry Week. *And, "I firmly believe my job is to walk around with a can of water in one hand and a can of fertilizer in the other and to make things flourish," is how he phrased it to writer Ken Auletta. It is short and sweet, but you know what he means. You know that he knows exactly what he is doing and why. Such clarity motivates. (Some might say that spreading fertilizer is too simplistic a job description for the CEO of GE, but try another Welch line to bring things back to a less poetical basis: "What counts is what you deliver."[16])*

♦ *Motivate through energy. Andrew Campbell, Michael Goold and Marcus Alexander note in* Corporate-Level Strategy *that Welch's "personal energy has driven the company forward, and his grasp of the issues in the various businesses is remarkable."[17] Energy drives people forward. If you will, they can.*

♦ *Change it. Nothing must stay the same. From the downsizing of the 1980s to Work-Out and Six Sigma, Welch has determined that nothing at GE will remain as it was. The company moves constantly.*

NOTES

1 Peters, Tom, *Liberation Management*, Knopf, New York, 1992.

2 Landro, Laura, "GE's wizards turning from the bottom line to share of the market," *Wall Street Journal*, July 12, 1982.

3 Hodgson, Phil and Crainer, Stuart, *What Do High Performance Managers Really Do?* FT/Pitman, London, 1993.

4 Jackson, Tony and Gowers, Andrew, "Big enough to make mistakes," *Financial Times*, December 21, 1995.

5 Gelman, Eric and Wang, Penelope, "Jack Welch: GE's live wire," *Newsweek*, December 23, 1985.

6 This section owes much to the work of my colleagues Randall P. White and Philip Hodgson.

7 Kotter, John, *The General Managers*, Free Press, New York, 1982.

8 White, Randall P., "Choosing leaders, not experts," in *Changing European Human Resource Practices*, The Conference Board, Report No. 1003, 1992.

9 General Electric Annual Report, 1985.

10 Byrne, John, "How Jack Welch runs GE," *Business Week*, June 8, 1998.

11 Lowe, Janet, *Jack Welch Speaks*, John Wiley & Sons, New York, 1998.

12 Lorenz, Christopher, "Quantum leaps in a dangerous game," *Financial Times*, September 22, 1993.

13 Pascale, Richard, *Managing on the Edge: How the Smartest Companies Use Conflict to Stay Ahead*, Touchstone Books, 1991.

14 Pascale, Richard, "Manoeuvres for the millennium," *Human Resources*, November–December 1996.

15 Pascale, Richard, Millemann, Mark and Gioja, Linda, "Changing the way we change," *Harvard Business Review*, November–December 1997.

16 Byrne, John, "How Jack Welch runs GE."

17 Campbell, Andrew, Goold, Michael and Alexander, Marcus, *Corporate-Level Strategy*, John Wiley & Sons, New York, 1994.

Think Service

Our job is to sell more than just the box.

Jack Welch[1]

GET INTIMATE

For most of the twentieth century Western business-es have concentrated on selling boxes, plain and unadorned. Businesses focused on producing as many as possible as efficiently as they could. They did not embrace quality and customer service until the 1980s. Even then, inspiration came in the form of an NBC television program about the work of quality guru W. Edwards Deming rather than from some remarkable corporate insight. Then quality took off. Deming was feted. Suddenly, Western managers were seeking out every morsel of information about quality management and quality systems they could find. By 1984 there were over 3000 quality circles in American companies and many thousands of others appearing throughout the Western world. A deluge of books, reports, conferences, seminars and initiatives followed. Quality circles led to

TQM; just-in-time led to lean production and, in turn, to reengineering.

After this mountain of books and reports on the subject, you might have thought that quality and customer service would be perfectly understood and brilliantly practiced. Look around or think about your recent service encounters. Clearly, excellence remains elusive.

The problem, say Peter Kolesar, Garrett Van Ryzin and Wayne Cutler (two Columbia University academics and a consultant), is that the "industrialization of services" overlooks the degree of personal interaction—"intimacy"—required to provide service excellence.[2] Their starting point is that "service is doing the work of your customer." "As a result, it requires a high level of contact, communication and co-ordination with your customers," write Kolesar, Van Ryzin and Cutler. There is, therefore, more to service than mere efficiency. Industrial-style service efficiency (of which McDonald's is the paragon) too easily slips into impersonal inflexibility.

To avoid these pitfalls they suggest companies aspire to "industrialized intimacy." This needs to be based around seven fundamental principles. First is the self-explanatory "know your customer"—easily understood but often not very well practiced. Two, "strive for one-and-done servicing." By this they mean that companies should seek to condense the interaction with their customers to involve the minimum numbers of people and processes. Numerous "hand-offs" from one person to another irritate rather than serve. Three, "promote value-enhancing self-servicing"—use technology (such as the Internet) to allow customers to do more for themselves if they choose to do so. Four, "provide one-stop shopping"—if a company really does understand its customers it can provide other associated services. Five, "engineer competency into service delivery"—"Service competence must be institutionalized" with systems built around service excellence rather than relying on the competence of individuals. Six, "let customers design the product"—customers increasingly require

What customers really, really want:

"Most customers do not want feigned friendship from their providers. What they demand, simply, is competent, convenient, no-hassle delivery of only those services they value— all at a reasonable price."

the flexibility to tailor a bundle of products or services to their specific needs. Finally, "build long-term customer relationships."

Inevitably, all of this is easier said than delivered. Kolesar, Van Ryzin and Cutler conclude: "Most customers do not want feigned friendship from their providers. What they demand, simply, is competent, convenient, no-hassle delivery of only those services they value—all at a reasonable price." Simple, really.

The move from industrialized service to customer intimacy is what Jack Welch has sought to achieve at GE. When he took over, GE's attitude to customer service was typical of a traditional manufacturer. "At one time, GE executives spent more time on company politics than they did on actual business. People said that GE operated with its face to the CEO and its ass to the customer," Welch quipped.[3]

Welch has turned things around. He has done so in a number of ways:

1. Developing the softer side of GE's businesses

GE has moved from being a manufacturer to being a manufacturing and service business. In 1998 more than two-thirds of GE's revenues will come from financial, information and product services. Central to this transformation has been the development of its financial services operation.

As a new service, GE Capital has made the most of GE's strengths in other channels. By using the company's triple-A credit rating, it has gained financial power its competitors can only dream of. Its base remains GE customers—retailers and end consumers. Beginning by providing financing for GE equipment customers, GE Capital has become the largest issuer of private label credit cards for retailers and others. "We're trying to develop a culture that says the world is the marketplace—don't make distinctions by country. The distinction remains the type of customer, not the country," says GE Capital chairman, Gary Wendt. "The private label credit card business is really a marketing arm for retailers—we spend as much time dissecting customers' buying habits as their creditworthiness."

In the not too distant future it is possible that GE Capital, which finances everything from washing machines to jet engines, will make more money than all the rest of the company's businesses combined. "GE Capital could get to be 50 percent-plus of the company," Welch has said.[4]

In 1996, GE Capital made after-tax profits of $2.8 billion on revenues of $33 billion. Of U.S. financial services businesses, only Citicorp, the American International Group and Bank America earned more.

2. Making multiple channels work

GE has worked hard at sustaining a variety of customer channels. It has developed better means of servicing and meeting the needs of smaller retail outlets to make their businesses sustainable in the face of intensifying competition from big retailers such as Circuit City.

In order to make smaller retailers more viable GE developed a distribution system involving five different mixing warehouses and 76 locations where products can be delivered to the retailer or end user. Its logistics network delivers one- to two-day delivery service. This allows retailers to reduce inventory so they only need display models. For the retailers this is a major leap forward, because inventory usually ties up most of their assets. In addition, retailers are given the opportunity to take advantage of business loans and store remodeling kits as well as software to help them manage their stores more efficiently.

GE has effectively positioned itself as the retailer's partner rather than as simply a supplier and has made the small retail sales channel viable and sustainable. By providing quicker service, GE made the channel more economically attractive and split the gains with the retailers.

3. Developing customer knowledge

GE has explored changing customer expectations in great depth. GE's customer service help desk, the GE Answer Center, has been used to help gather valuable market research on evolving product and service preferences.

4. The Six Sigma initiative

In 1995 GE calculated that it was averaging 35,000 defects per million operations. This was a good performance if compared to other companies: It rated around 3.5 sigma. Jack Welch called on the company to reach six sigma.

Six Sigma was the third stage of Welch's corporate revolution. It was taken directly from the quality textbook. "Quality is not something you install like a new carpet or a set of bookshelves. You implant it. Quality is something you work at. It is a learning process," said W. Edwards Deming.[5] Quality, in Deming's eyes, was not the preserve of the few but the responsibility of all. He repeatedly said that management was 90 percent of the problem.

Six Sigma was regarded by GE as the logical development from Work-Out. The people were now involved. Now was the time to up the standards. The company's 1997 Annual Report explained: "After a decade of Work-Out, most of the old bureaucracy and the boundaries among us have been demolished. (We are, however, aware that bureaucracy is the Dracula of institutional behavior, and will rise again and again, requiring everyone in the organization to reflexively pound stakes through its reappearances.)"

In characteristic GE fashion, Six Sigma was an idea that already worked elsewhere. Ever the corporate magpies, GE simply transplanted the idea to its own organization. It did so with customary frankness: "We didn't invent Six Sigma—we learned it. Motorola pioneered it and Allied Signal successfully embraced it. The experience of these two companies, which they shared with us, made the launch of our initiative much simpler and faster."[6] If only the others could be so commonsensical.

What was different about Six Sigma was that it was not the usual superficial quality campaign. The lead came directly from the top. "This is not about sloganeering or bureaucracy or filling out forms. It finally gives us a route to get to the control function, the hardest thing to do in a corporation," Welch said.[7] Even so, Six Sigma comes laden with the usual acronyms: CTQs (critical to quality characteristics); DPMOs (defects per million opportunities) and SPC (statistical process control).

The GE board has called Six Sigma "the centerpiece of our dreams and aspirations for this great company." It is, they say, "a disciplined methodology led and taught by highly trained GE employees called Master Black belts and Black belts." To date the company has trained 4000 full-time Black belts and Master Black belts and 60,000 Green belt part-time project leaders.

Six Sigma revolves around five basic activities:

♦ defining,
♦ measuring,
♦ analyzing,
♦ improving, and
♦ controlling processes.

Six Sigma reaped immediate benefits. GE's operating margins exceeded 15 percent during 1997; previously they had remained around 10 percent. GE calculates that Six Sigma delivered more than $300 million to its 1997 operating income. During 1997, GE increased its calculation of the money it saved through its Six Sigma program—from $400 to $650 million. By the year 2000 one analyst expects GE's savings to be over $6 billion.[8] Not bad for a secondhand idea.

THINK SERVICE

♦ **Leverage service.** *Once upon a time, GE sold boxes. You went to your friendly retailer and bought a washing machine. That was that. Now, the washing machine is only a lure to get you into the GE empire of service. You buy the washing machine with credit from GE's very own credit company in a store kitted out at GE's expense. Your numbers and details are fed in. You walk out with the hardware while GE's software cranks into action. The box is increasingly incidental.*

♦ **Lead quality initiatives from the top.** *Six Sigma has worked partly because Jack Welch and the GE broad have backed it with their lives. They espouse it at every opportunity. They believe in it. And, most of all, they are a part of it.*

♦ **Steal the best ideas.** *In business originality is overrated. History is littered with the failed businesses of people who had the ideas first but didn't know what to do with them or how to run a business. GE took Six Sigma—quite openly—from the experiences of Motorola and Allied Signal. But it didn't take it wholesale. It moulded and shaped it to GE's own expectations and aspirations.*

♦ **Do it yourself.** *Consultants aren't all bad—despite what you might read. But it is noticeable that GE does things for itself. It doesn't bring in a consulting firm with its own quality package and then wait for quality to happen. It doesn't buy a shiny new carpet and then put it down on top of the dirt.*

NOTES

1   Smart, Tim, "Jack Welch's encore," *Business Week,* October 28, 1996.

2   Kolesar, Peter, Van Ryzin, Garrett and Cutler, Wayne, "Creating customer value," *Strategy & Business,* third quarter, 1998.

3   Tichy, Noel and Sherman, Stratford, *Control Your Destiny or Someone Else Will,* Doubleday Currency, New York, 1993.

4   Waters, Richard, "Too big for its booties," *Financial Times,* October 9, 1997.

5   Crainer, Stuart, *The Ultimate Business Guru Book,* Capstone, Oxford, 1998.

6   General Electric Annual Report, 1997.

7   Conlin, Michelle, "Revealed at last: the secret of Jack Welch's success," *Forbes,* January 26, 1998.

8   Conlin, Michelle, "Revealed at last: the secret of Jack Welch's success," *Forbes,* January 26, 1998.

Forget the Past;
Love the Future

*The fact that Welch has no institutional memory
and doesn't allow others to nurture their own is
one of GE's most valuable assets.*

Adrian Slywotzky[1]

THE FUTURE BEGINS AT THE TOP

Bogged down in meetings with analysts shouting for short-term results, senior managers are tempted to manage in the present and wait for the future to take care of itself.

However, putting your head above the parapet has never been more important. The further you look the better your future is likely to be. According to strategy guru Gary Hamel, companies that view change as an internal matter are liable to be left behind. Instead they need to look outside of their industry boundaries. Hamel calculates that if you want to see the future coming, 80 percent of the learning will take place outside company boundaries. Looking outside is not something companies are very good at. "The good news is that companies in most industries are blind in the same way," says Hamel. "There is no inevitability about the future. There is no proprietary data about

"There is no inevitability about the future. There is no proprietary data about the future. The goal is to imagine what you can make happen."

the future. The goal is to imagine what you can make happen."[2] The trouble is that most executives left their imagination back in high school. Who needs imagination when you've got a dossier of hard facts to show?

The answer comes from Hamel, who argues that there are four preconditions for wealth-creating strategies. First, a company must have "new passions." People inside the organization must care deeply about the future. Whether you like him or loathe him, you can't deny that Jack Welch is passionate about the future of GE. He cares.

Second, wealth creation requires "new voices." In many companies Hamel observes "a lack of genetic diversity. Young people are largely disenfranchised from discussions of strategy. We need a hierarchy of imagination, not experience. Among the people who work on strategy in organizations and the theorists, a huge proportion, perhaps 95 percent, are economists and engineers who share a mechanistic view of strategy. Where are the theorists, the anthropologists to give broader and fresher insights?" Jack Welch didn't have to bring in the anthropologists: He just let the GE workers loose through Work-Out.

Third, Hamel calls for "new conversations." Instead of having the same five people talking to the same five people for the fifth year in a row, more people need to become involved in the process of strategy creation. Again, Work-Out created new conversations within GE.

Finally, there is a need for "new perspectives." "You cannot make people any smarter but you can give them new lenses," says Hamel. "Only non-linear strategies will create new wealth."

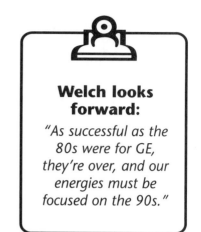

There are, of course, other options. Many will continue to ignore Hamel's call for a revolution in favor of easy route. "There is a lot of talk about creating shareholders' wealth. It is not a hard thing to do. Just find a 60-year-old CEO and set a 65-year-old retirement age and then guarantee a salary based on the share price growing." The trouble is that it is here, at the stock-option-packed top of the organization, that change needs to begin. "What we need is not visionaries but activists. We need antidotes to *Dilbert*," Hamel proclaims.

Welch fits the bill. His continual focus is on the future. The past is history. At the company's 1990 Annual General Meeting, Welch pronounced: "As successful as the 80s were for GE, they're over, and our energies must be focused on the 90s."[3] Yesterday's achievements will mean nothing tomorrow.

Forget the past. What's happening today and tomorrow is more important. Welch argues that Work-Out was part of this process: "Work-Out has a practical and an intellectual goal. The practical objective is to get rid of thousands of bad habits accumulated since the creation of GE. How would you like to move from a house after 112 years? Think of what would be in the closets and the attic—those shoes that you'll wear to paint next spring, even though you know you'll never paint again. We've got 112 years of closets and attics in this company. We want to flush them out, to start with a brand-new house with empty closets, to begin the whole game again."[4] The organization—any organization—has to shift, develop and move forward or face becoming immersed and immobilized in the past.

ENVISION THE FUTURE

GE hasn't moved blindly into the future. It has envisioned the future and then sought to create it.

"We didn't argue what the computer should be, we all knew what the computer should be. Our job was to go out and make it work," commented one of the design engineers on the Apple Macintosh team. Such clarity of purpose is rare, for all the mission statements and visionary exhortations by executives in annual reports.

Peter Drucker cut to the heart of the problem in a comparison of Japanese and Western attitudes. "One of the greatest differences between the Japanese and Europeans and Americans is that they don't take their mission for granted. They start off with 'What are we trying to do?' Not, 'How do we do it?'"

Having a mobile yet clear and committed vision is critical in effective leadership. It unites and enables different teams, departments and individuals to forget their differences and work toward a strong, common goal. It is not a public relations exercise or a derided mission statement pinned on a factory notice board. It is a real and living raison d'etre.

Vision is interpreted by leading British businessman Sir Adrian Cadbury as direction: "It is a sense of direction that we need to keep in mind when assessing leadership. The directional sense of leaders is more important than their powers of leadership and the two attributes do not necessarily go together . . . Many have the desire to lead or the gift of leadership, but fewer, far fewer . . . combine them with vision and sound judgement. If you are told that a business is a going concern, it is as well to ascertain for yourself in which direction it is going."[5]

Cadbury goes on to examine the real role of vision: "Vision is central to ensuring that everyone in an organization knows what the goals of the enterprise are and how their particular job contributes to them. In addition, a sense of vision is what inspires people to feel both that the company's aims are their aims and that they are worthy of achievement. Companies are in business to achieve goals. The leader's task is to determine those goals, to communicate them and to win commitment to them."

Jack Welch sees creating and communicating a vision for the company as a central part of his job: "Good business leaders create a vision. They articulate the vision, passionately own the vision, and relentlessly drive it to completion. Above all else, good leaders are open. They go up, down, and around their organization to reach people. They don't stick to established channels. They're informal. They're straight with people. They make a religion out of being accessible. They never get bored telling their story."[6]

In Welch's hands, vision is tangible instead of ethereal, real instead of a dream.

Welch on vision:
"Good business leaders create a vision. They articulate the vision, passionately own the vision, and relentlessly drive it to completion."

EMBRACE TECHNOLOGY

The hyperbole surrounding the technological explosion of the last decade has tended to obscure a number of important facts. First, senior executives are often highly skeptical. They may not be Luddites, but they are far from comfortable with IT. Second, IT is a tool rather than a cure for all known organizational ills. Third, IT needs to be made to work; companies cannot just lie back and think of the balance sheet.

Some companies appear to understand. Jack Welch has identified information systems as a top priority for GE. Benetton manages its retail chain via computer. Others are less convinced. "We are starting to see a new breed of manager that recognizes the importance of IT. But most still don't," laments Booz-Allen & Hamilton consultant, Charles Callahan.[7]

IT writer Victoria Griffith, writing in *Strategy & Business,* suggests that IT needs to be integrated into business strategy. IT should be presented as a top priority and supported as such throughout the organization. This involves bringing IT personnel into the senior management cadre, a move that often requires overturning long-held prejudices. "CIOs should drop the jargon and talk about revenue-producing initiatives. CEOs must listen," advocates Griffith with commendable gusto. She suggests that an IT chief with a business background is preferable to one with an engineering perspective. Finally, she argues that instead of being measured by costs, IT success should be measured by profits. Instead of being seen as a creator of costs, IT needs to be perceived as a driver and creator of revenue. Indeed, it needs to be regarded as part of the business rather than as an adjunct to it.

Jack Welch has enthusiastically embraced technology. GE's Call Center leads the way. GE is at the forefront of doing business via the Internet. "General Electric is determined to be the beneficiary, not the victim, of the microelectronics revolution. You must all advance our technological renaissance," Welch told GE employees in 1981.[8] The future is here.

READING THE FUTURE

In his 1982 book, Megatrends, *futurist John Naisbitt identified ten "critical restructurings." While some have proved accurate predictions of what has happened in intervening years, others have proved less accurate. However, those that follow reflect the changes Jack Welch has brought about at GE:*

♦ *"Although we continue to think we live in an industrial society, we have in fact changed to an economy based on the creation and distribution of information," wrote Naisbitt. This has become accepted and is now a truism. In the early 1980s, however, traditional issues, such as production methods, still held sway. Naisbitt was ahead of the game. The technological possibilities in information exchange and transfer were contemplated by a small group in West coast laboratories, and by Jack Welch, who has moved GE remorselessly away from manufacturing to service.*

♦ *"We are moving in the dual directions of high-tech/high-touch, matching each new technology with a compensatory human response." This is a theme Naisbitt has returned to and developed in more recent years. "The acceleration of technological progress has created an urgent need for a counter*

---

ballast—for high-touch experiences. Heart trans-
plants have led to new interest in family doctors and
neighborhood clinics; jet airplanes have resulted in
more face-to-face meetings. High-touch is about get-
ting back to a human scale," he says. "All change is
local and bottom-up . . . If you keep track of local
events, you can see the shifting patterns. Also,
remember that high-tech/high-touch isn't an
either/or decision. You can't stop technological
progress, but by the same token, you can hardly go
wrong with a high-touch response. Give out your
home phone number. Send a handwritten letter.
FedEx has all the reliability and efficiency of modern
electronics, but its success is built on a form of high-
touch: hand delivery." Back to service once again.
Welch kept GE in touch with smaller retailers and
many of the changes he has pushed through are to
enable GE to deliver personal service more efficiently.

♦ *"No longer do we have the luxury of operating within*
an isolated, self-sufficient, national economic system;
we must now acknowledge that we are part of a
global economy. We have begun to let go of the idea
that the U.S. is and must remain the world's industrial
leader as we move on to other tasks." Naisbitt was
right to identify the emergence of globalization as a
powerful force. His perception of a change in
America's perception of itself is open to doubt.
Naisbitt has gone on to explore what he calls the
"global paradox" which he believes is that, "The big-
ger the world economy, the more powerful its smallest
player." GE has cemented its global operations.
Welch's quest for a boundaryless organization has
made it easier for GE people to share knowledge and
experience, no matter where they are.

♦ *"We are restructuring from a society run by short-*
term considerations and rewards in favor of dealing

with things in much longer-term time frames." There is little evidence, some 16 years on, that this trend has become a reality. At GE, however, long-term considerations have held sway throughout the century. The company has never dispensed with a CEO who has made short-term errors. The long-term success of the company is all-important.

* *"In cities and states, in small organizations and subdivisions, we have rediscovered the ability to act innovatively and to achieve results—from the bottom up." Naisbitt anticipated the fashion in the late 1980s and early 1990s for empowerment with responsibility being spread more evenly throughout organizations rather than centered on a coterie of managers. Welch's Work-Out program is one of the most potent demonstrations of empowerment in practice anywhere in the corporate world.*

* *"We are giving up our dependence on hierarchical structures in favor of informal networks. This will be especially important to the business community." This has become one of the great trends of the last decade as networks are developed in a bewildering variety of ways—with suppliers, between competitors, internally, globally. Technology has enabled the creation of networks never previously anticipated, with important repercussions. "When everyone hears about everything at the same time, everyone else hears about it, and we all know that. Instantly. But we still have the same old system. So . . . we're going through a big period of correction," says Naisbitt.[9] Linked to this is the entire question of speed, which Naisbitt identified early on as a competitive weapon. "Economies of scale are giving way to economies of scope, finding the right size for synergy, market flexibility, and above all, speed," he says in* The Global Paradox. *This is the world according to Jack Welch.*

FORGET THE PAST; LOVE THE FUTURE

+ *Make the future today.* *"Tomorrow is our permanent address,"* said Marshall McLuhan. Jack Welch has put the future on GE's agenda. *Many executives and organizations find themselves unable to do so. Either the present is too desperately captivating or the future too daunting. But a company either decides to influence and dictate the future or sits down and lets it happen. Only one of these courses is likely to bring long-term success to its business.*

+ *Get ready but be flexible.* *"There are many methods for predicting the future. For example, you can read horoscopes, tea leaves, tarot cards or crystal balls. Collectively, these methods are known as* nutty methods. *Or you can put well-researched facts into sophisticated computer models, more commonly referred to as a* complete waste of time," *says* Dilbert *creator* Scott Adams. *Plan all you like, but you have to be prepared to change as you go along. Your mission cannot be fixed but must constantly change.*

+ *The future is going to be different.* *"You can never plan the future by the past,"* said Edmund Burke. *In this age of speed, turbulence and continuous development you can be sure that the future will be unlike the past in as many ways as can be imagined.*

+ *Look outside. Any environment, however stimulating in the short term, is constraining. Leaders have to be able to look over the walls, to look outside for new perspectives, examples and inspirations. Great leaders are perpetually searching for new perspectives, fresh insights, more information and more effective methods of delivering their vision. Perhaps it is eccentricity that allows leaders to take an alternative view. They are constantly able to appreciate and adopt a differ-*

ent, broader, more sensitive or more inspiring perspective on a particular situation or issue.

♦ *Utilize technology but don't fall in love with it. Technology is a liberating force. It can make people and organizations more efficient. But it will only do so, if it is approached in a business-like manner. Only fools rush in.*

♦ *Be optimistic. There are plenty of dire predictions. There is no example of company ever succeeding in the future when managed by people who are pessimistic about the possibilities and potential. Jack Welch is positive and relentlessly optimistic. He sees potential for growth and discovery and efficiency everywhere he looks.*

NOTES

1   Slywotzky, Adrian, *Value Migration*, Harvard Business School Press, Boston, 1996.

2   Crainer, Stuart, *The Ultimate Business Guru Book*, Capstone, Oxford, 1998.

3   General Electric Annual General Meeting, 1990.

4   Tichy, Noel and Charan, Ram, "Speed, simplicity and self-confidence," *Harvard Business Review,* September–October 1989.

5   Cadbury, Sir Adrian, *Leaders on Leadership*, Institute of Management, London, 1996.

6   Tichy, Noel and Charan, Ram, "Speed, simplicity and self-confidence," *Harvard Business Review*, September-October 1989.

7   Griffith, Victoria, "Making Information Technology Strategic," *Strategy & Business*, fourth quarter, 1997.

8   "Passing the torch," *Monogram*, January–February 1981.

9   Interview with John Naisbitt, *Star Tribune*, November 1996.

6
Learn and Lead

The interesting quality of Jack Welch is that he is an ever-growing, ever-evolving character. Welch of the early 1980s regarded terms like empowerment and transformation as California talk.

RICHARD PASCALE[1]

THE NEW MODEL LEADER

"Our traditional views of leaders—as special people who set the direction, make the key decisions, and energize the troops—are deeply rooted in an individualistic and non-systemic worldview. Especially in the West, leaders are heroes—great men (and occasionally women) who *rise to the fore* in times of crises," laments MIT's Peter Senge. "Our prevailing leadership myths are still captured by the image of the captain of the cavalry leading the charge to rescue the settlers from the attacking Indians. So long as such myths prevail, they reinforce a focus on short-term events and charismatic heroes rather than on systemic forces and collective learning. At its heart, the traditional view of leadership is based on assumptions of people's powerlessness, their lack of personal vision and inability to master the forces of change, deficits which can be remedied only by a few great leaders."

The business leader's role is changing. Traditional views on leadership tended to concentrate on vision and charisma. Today, the message seems to be that charisma is no longer enough to carry leaders through—leaders with strong personalities are as likely to bite the corporate dust (as Bob Horton found to his cost at BP, John Akers at IBM, even Al Dunlap). The new model leaders include people like Percy Barnevik at Asea Brown Boveri, Virgin's Richard Branson and Jack Welch.

At the same time as the leader's role has been transformed, leadership has become more complex and arguably even more critical to success. Leaders must ensure that high performance levels are achieved and sustained. At the same time, they must handle growing complexity and ambiguity; initiate and lead change processes; ensure that the organization and its processes constantly develop; and see that people within the company are motivated, developed and rewarded to produce outstanding results. The leader is no longer simply an isolated individual at the top of the organization. Indeed, the very individualism associated with leadership is also now a bone of contention. The people we tend to think of as leaders— from Napoleon to Margaret Thatcher—are not exactly renowned for their team-working skills. But these are exactly the skills all-important for contemporary leaders. New business leaders have to be veritable renaissance men and women.

"In some cases, the needs of a situation bring to the fore individuals with unique qualities or values; however, most leaders have to fit their skills, experience and vision to a particular time and place," says psychologist Robert Sharrock of YSC. "Today's leaders have to be pragmatic and flexible to survive. Increasingly, this means being people rather than task-oriented. The 'great man' theory about leadership rarely applies—if teams are what make businesses run, then we have to look beyond individual leaders to groups of people with a variety of leadership skills."[2]

Indeed, the pendulum has swung so far that there is growing interest in the study of followers. Once the humble foot soldier was ignored as commentators sought out the general. Now the foot soldiers are encouraged to voice their opinions and shape how the organization works. "Followers are becoming more powerful. It is now common for the performance of bosses to be scrutinized and appraised by their corporate followers. This, of course, means that leaders have to actively seek the support of their followers in a way they would never have previously contemplated," says Robert Sharrock.

Phil Hodgson of the U.K.'s Ashridge Management College has analyzed a number of business leaders. His conclusion is that the old models of leadership are no longer appropriate. "Generally, the managers had outgrown the notion of the individualistic leader. Instead, they regarded leadership as a question of drawing people and disparate parts of the organization together in a way that made individuals and the organization more effective."[3] He concludes that the new leaders must add value as coaches, mentors and prob-

The new leaders must add value as coaches, mentors and problem solvers; must allow people to accept credit for success and responsibility for failure; and must continually evaluate and enhance their own leadership roles.

lem solvers; must allow people to accept credit for success and responsibility for failure; and must continually evaluate and enhance their own leadership roles. "They don't follow rigid or orthodox role models, but prefer to nurture their own unique leadership styles," he says. "And, they don't do people's jobs for them or put their faith in developing a personality cult." The new recipe for leadership, says Hodgson, centers on five key areas: learning, energy, simplicity, focus and inner sense.

The magic that sets leaders apart has been examined by INSEAD leadership expert Manfred Kets de Vries. "They go beyond narrow definitions. They have an ability to excite people in their organizations," he says. "They also work extremely hard—leading by example is not dead—and are highly resistant to stress. Also, leaders . . . are very aware of what their failings are. They make sure that they find good people who can fill these areas."[4]

In the age of empowerment, the ability to delegate effectively is critically important. "Empowerment and leadership are not mutually exclusive," says de Vries. "The trouble is that many executives feel it is good to have control. They become addicted to power—and that is what kills companies."

Ron Heifetz of Harvard Business School and consultant Don Laurie contend that corporate leaders and organizations are now facing "adaptive challenges."[5] The technical know-how to meet these challenges often exists, but that does not necessarily make life any easier. "Adaptive work is required when our deeply held beliefs are challenged, when the values that made us successful become less relevant, and when legitimate yet competing perspectives emerge," they write.

Adaptive work requires leadership, a skill in perennial short supply. Heifetz and Laurie suggest that the kind of leadership best suited to adaptive change is based on six principles. First is what they label "getting on the balcony." Business leaders must be able to involve themselves in the nitty-gritty while maintaining an overall perspective. This is the prerequisite for success. Think how Jack Welch combines repeated emphasis on the GE vision with keeping in touch with the nitty-gritty of the business and taking time out to check on progress and performance and approve who fills managerial positions.

The second leadership skill lies in identifying the adaptive challenge. This is a somewhat nebulous term for getting beneath the surface and really identifying where cultural problems lie. The third facet is regulating distress. The leader must recognize that change causes stress and distress. Moving too quickly or not giving people an opportunity to relieve the pressure is counterproductive. Fourth, leaders must "maintain disciplined attention." "People need leadership to help them maintain their focus on the tough questions. Disciplined attention is the currency of leadership," Heifetz and Laurie write. Leaders steer people to confront the really tough questions they would rather ignore.

The final two principles of adaptive leadership are closely linked: "give the work back to people" and "protect voices of leadership from below." People must be involved in any process of change and must be allowed to express their opinions, even if they are discordant. What links all these elements is the perpetual need for questioning. "Leaders do not need to know all the answers. They do need to ask the right questions," say Heifetz and Laurie, neatly concluding that, "One can lead with no more than a question in hand."

Distilling all these points down, the new model leader is characterized by the following.

Willingness to make mistakes and admit fallibility

Business leaders are no longer regarded as infallible. The pedestal has been removed. Leaders are human. They make mistakes.

In 1986 GE bought 80 percent of Kidder Peabody for $600 million. The Kidder debacle cost GE $1.2 billion. "I've rewarded failures by giving out awards to people when they've failed, because they took a swing," says Jack Welch. "Keep taking swings. I teach a course at Crotonville for six hours—four to six hours—on leadership. I always say, if the chairman can buy Kidder Peabody and mess it up, you can do about anything. It was on the front page of the *Wall Street Journal* 19 times. Now, if the chairman can do that and still survive, you ought to be able to take swings everywhere. You can hardly do worse."[6]

Welch claims to have built a culture in which failure is accepted as a positive thing. "Punishing failure assures that no one dares," he contends.[7] The emphasis is on taking risks and learning from them if things go wrong.

This message is also hitting home elsewhere in industry. The CEO of one major U.S. corporation handed out awards for Best Failures during his senior executive forum. Jaws dropped at the very thought. This represented a major cultural shift in that only a year before failures—especially big or public ones—were to be hidden, not celebrated.

To a large extent this is simply recognizing that the most intensive learning experiences tend to occur when we fail rather than when we succeed. "Most of the things I have learnt were not learned formally but through accidents and failure. I learned from small catastrophes," admits Charles Handy, author of *The Age of Unreason*.[8] Handy is not alone. Most of us learn in just such a haphazard and occasionally unhappy way. If there were awards for Best Failures we would have a large number to choose from.

Indeed, one U.K. newspaper ran a weekly column entitled "My biggest mistake." It was riveting reading as manager after manager confessed to some appalling misjudgment. It was notable that all the mistakes were made in prehistoric times—the executives couldn't admit to recent errors of judgment—and that their vital lessons stayed with the executives. In many cases they haunted them. A mistake made was a lesson learned and remembered.

We could all write similar articles. Perhaps we should, regularly. Yet though we are often shaken by our failures, too often we are not stirred from our habitual behavior. We don't want to stand out by getting it wrong. We merge with the crowd. Fear of failure is a fundamental instinct, one that organizations only serve to magnify.

In organizations, fear of failure becomes a survival instinct. We go into organizations and we learn and are taught by the organization how to operate. If you start a job on the checkout counter of a retail chain, you will spend a day watching videos (it's cheap and doesn't waste valuable managerial time) about the way the corporation works, its values and ways of doing things. Good idea, but it is prescriptive. It won't tell us about what happens when things go wrong—except that if they go too wrong you will be fired.

Another retail chain has a better idea. It throws staff in at the deep end by giving them a day at the counter to see how they deal with real customers. Then it can make a decision about whether someone is really right for the job.

Work at Decision Research, a company based in Eugene, Oregon that studies risk management strategies, suggests that people are more likely to accept risks that they perceive as voluntarily undertaken, controllable, understandable and equally distributed. Conversely, people are less willing to take on risks that they don't understand and that are unfairly distributed.[9]

Learning

"When I stop learning something new and start talking about the past versus the future, I will go," says Jack Welch.[10] Today's leaders must lead *and* learn. This is clearly a substantial change and an even more substantial challenge.

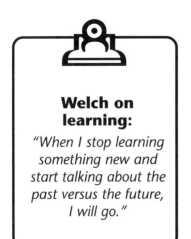

Welch on learning:

"When I stop learning something new and start talking about the past versus the future, I will go."

Many business leaders are handicapped by a mental model that insists that learning is a passive activity. Also, most top managers are used to displaying their self-confidence and competence rather than admitting they feel insecure, vulnerable or anxious. Most are good at parading their strengths and rarely have the opportunity—or willingness—to discuss their weaknesses with people who understand the pressures but have no direct business relationship with them.

Learning involves taking a risk and taking risks makes us vulnerable. People are afraid to make themselves more vulnerable, to expose themselves to potential loss of face, loss of opportunity or simply loss. As a result, executives develop what has been accurately labeled the myth of mastery. By steering clear of trouble spots and situations that make them vulnerable, executives begin to believe that they are invincible.

Mastering the soft stuff

Macho leadership is dead. "We've got to take out the boss element. We're going to win on our ideas, not by whips and chains," says Jack Welch, a master of the soft skills of leadership.[11] He coaches. He communicates. "Increasingly CEOs and directors have to be coaches. They need to coach their managers. They need to help people to develop," says Brian Chernett, founder and executive chairman of the Academy for Chief Executives. "The skill of being able to influence people is the most important skill for those at the top. The trouble is that such soft skills are anathema to many. Sometimes you have to disguise them—as a modeling process or as learning from people who are highly successful."[12]

Welch on ideas:

"We've got to take out the boss element. We're going to win on our ideas, not by whips and chains."

Involving people

Says Jack Welch: "I hope you understand that business is a series of trial-and-error. It's not a

THE ROOTS OF WORK-OUT

GE's Work-Out has received plaudits as a groundbreaking idea. In fact, like most managerial ideas, it is simply a new take on an old idea. The idea in this case is Action Learning. This was the brainchild of the idiosyncratic British academic Reg Revans. Revans created a simple equation: $L = P + Q$. Learning occurs through a combination of programmed knowledge (P) and the ability to ask insightful questions (Q). "The essence of action learning is to become better acquainted with the self by trying to observe what one may actually do, to trace the reasons for attempting it and the consequences of what one seemed to be doing," he says.[14]

While programmed knowledge is one-dimensional and rigid, the ability to ask questions opens up other dimensions and is free-flowing. Revans argues that educational institutions remain fixated with programmed knowledge instead of encouraging students to ask questions and roam widely around a subject.

The structure linking the two elements is the small team or set. "The central idea of this approach to human development, at all levels, in all cultures and for all purposes, is today that of the set, or small group of comrades in adversity, striving to learn with and from each other as they confess failures and expand on victories," writes Revans in Action Learning.

Action learning is the antithesis of the traditional approach to developing managers. "You must seek to understand each other's problems and develop a sense of responsibility for each other through working in small groups," says Revans.

The wide-ranging scope of action learning and the eclectic mind of Revans make it clear that action learning is no quick fix. It requires a fundamental change in thinking.

There are some suggestions that action learning may be gaining in popularity. Among its supporters are Lord Weinstock and Sir Peter Parker. GE's Work-Out is a form of action learning. It uses action teams to tackle particular problems. This ad hoc *approach carries the proviso that the teams do not necessarily understand what they have learned.*

great science. Mistakes are made. It's just moving the ball forward, and nobody has any great formula. If we have any one formula, it's that we believe that you've got to involve everyone in the game. You can't let any one mind guard the game. And we work on that every day, and everybody has to play, and more people [have to] share in the victory of the game."[13]

Welch has succeeded in involving people—empowering in management jargon—in the future of GE. The chief element in achieving this was the Work-Out program, which gave people a voice, often for the first time and, most importantly, a voice that was clearly listened to.

NOTES

1 Pascale, Richard, *Managing on the Edge*, Simon & Schuster, New York, 1990.

2 Author interview.

3 Author interview.

4 Author interview.

5 Heifetz, Ronald and Laurie, Donald L., "The work of leadership," *Harvard Business Review*, January–February 1997.

6 Lowe, Janet, *Jack Welch Speaks*, John Wiley & Sons, New York, 1998.

7 Welch, John F., "Shun the incremental," *Financier*, July 1984.

8 Author interview.

9 Kleiner, K., "Beware experts carrying stigmas," *New Scientist*, October 21, 1995.

10 Hirata, Ikuo, "Moving toward small-company soul in a big-company body," *Nikkei Business*, February 21, 1994.

11 Stewart, Thomas, "GE keeps those ideas coming," *Fortune*, August 12, 1991.

12 Author interview.

13 Lowe, Janet, *Jack Welch Speaks*.

14 Author interview.

15 Crainer, Stuart (editor), *Leaders on Leadership*, Institute of Management, London, 1996.

LEARN AND LEAD

♦ *Add the human touch.* *Addressing the superintendents of his factories, the nineteenth-century businessman Robert Owen said: "Many of you have long experiences in your manufacturing operations of the advantages of substantial, well-contrived and well-executed machinery. If, then, due care as to the state of the machinery can produce such beneficial results, what may not be expected if you devote equal attention to your animate machines, which are far more wonderfully constructed?" The human touch is central to any leadership role. Marshaling, motivating and engaging everyone in the organization is one of the prime responsibilities of the leader. Jack Welch has the human touch.*

♦ *Learn and learn some more.* *"I am always ready to learn, although I do not always like being taught," said Sir Winston Churchill. Learning is now an integral part of executive leadership. The leader who does not learn will not survive.*

♦ *Set direction and build values.* *The leader needs to carry out a precarious balancing act. He or she has to set the long-term objectives and vision of an organization, yet has also to "connect" with people throughout the organization. There is a perpetual danger of becoming bogged down in minor, localized problems or, at the other extreme, becoming cut off from the lifeblood of the organization. Harold Macmillan was once asked what was the most difficult thing about being prime minister. "Events, my dear boy, events," he replied.*

In the past, the senior executive was expected to be deeply involved in every aspect of a company's activities. Expectations are changing. "If the people on the front line really are the keys to our success, then the manager's job is to help those people, the people that they serve," says Robert Haas, president and chief executive of Levi-Strauss. "That goes against the traditional assumption that the manager is in control. In the past, a manager was expected to know everything that was going on and to be deeply involved in subordinates' activities."[13]

The leader therefore sets the tone, establishes values and creates an example. "The tail trails the head. If the head moves fast, the tail will keep up the same pace. If the head is sluggish, the tail will droop," is how Japanese industrialist Konosuke Matsushita phrased this.

♦ **Change things.** "The leader's job is to help everyone see that the platform is burning, whether the flames are apparent or not. The process of change begins when people decide to take the flames seriously and manage by fact, and that means a brutal understanding of reality. You need to find out what the reality is so that you know what needs changing," says Larry Bossidy of Allied Signal. The leader is an agent provocateur, fanning the flames of change and enabling people to embrace and capitalize on change. "Leadership produces change. That is its primary function," says Harvard Business School's John Kotter.

♦ **Create tomorrow's leaders.** Ralph Nader said: "I start with the premise that the function of leadership is to produce more leaders, not more followers." As we have seen, Jack Welch invests heavily, in terms of both time and money, in creating and developing tomorrow's leaders.

No Bull

It is vital for the success of our companies that businessmen and women emerge as real leaders and demonstrate their ability to communicate effectively, internally and externally.

SIR COLIN MARSHALL, CHAIRMAN,
BRITISH AIRWAYS[1]

KISS

KISS—Keep It Simple, Stupid—is a perennially useful acronym, especially in management where obfuscation and bullshit reign. Jack Welch believes in KISS. "This isn't rocket science; we've chosen one of the world's more simple professions," he says. "Most global businesses have three or four critical competitors, and you know who they are. And there aren't that many things you can do with a business. It's not as if you're choosing 2000 options."[2]

Many would disagree. To them management and business appear appallingly complex. But Welch has an uncanny ability to simplify the complex. He simpli-

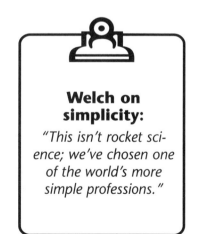

Welch on simplicity:

"This isn't rocket science; we've chosen one of the world's more simple professions."

fies to communicate. Welch realizes that in the modern business environment, communication is no longer a rigid, formal process. Instead, it has to be dynamic, powerful and immediate. "If we can simplify something we will. If we can make it simple we can communicate it easily to our people and people can understand, champion it and endeavor to take an active part on the program," said John Cahill when chief executive of the conglomerate BTR.[3]

This sort of directness is critical to successful communication. Jack Welch talks straight. A spade is a spade. "Welch says his mother taught him three important lessons: to communicate candidly, to face reality, and to control your own destiny," writes Janet Lowe in *Jack Welch Speaks*.[4]

Welch does not talk in management jargon. He is blunt. Speaking to the annual management conference of NBC executives in 1987, Welch said: "We're going to demand from you earnings growth every year. And don't give us any shrugs about that. Those are the rules of the road . . . You take charge of your destiny. If you don't, we will."[5] Does any other CEO talk to his execs like that?

COMMUNICATE CONTINUALLY

Jack Welch communicates continually. There is no let-up. He is continually talking and writing. He knows that a few scribbled words from him is a powerful message. It shows that he has taken the time, that the person matters. Often he says and writes the same thing. Like a presidential candidate with a stump speech, to get the message home he constantly repeats its essence. But he never appears bored by it.

Percy Barnevik of ABB estimates that he spends one-tenth of his time deciding on the strategy and the rest communicating it. Such a bias says a great deal about the critical importance of communication. It is not an indulgence or a distraction, but a must for any manager in any organization. Welch makes a similar dedication of his time.

In 1987 Welch spoke to GE employees: "We've learned a bit about what communication is not. It's not a speech like this or a videotape. It's not a plant newspaper. Real communication is an attitude, an environment. It's the most interactive of all processes. It requires countless hours of eyeball-to-eyeball back and forth. It involves more listening than talking. It is a constant, interactive process aimed at (creating) consensus."[6]

With Welch, communication is personal. He recognizes that a casual or short conversation with someone is more valuable than a few paragraphs in a company newsletter.

But not only does Jack Welch talk. He also listens. Communication, as Work-Out demonstrates, has to be two-way. "Charismatic leadership, contrary to popular belief, is not one of the features of successful companies. Instead, the common factor is leadership which is both forthright and listening. It is very assertive about standards and objectives, making clear that quality is non-negotiable and that customer service is genuinely and consistently the number one priority. At the same time the leadership not only encourages employees to give their views about how to improve quality, it actively listens to those views, acts on them and draws on the knowledge and experience of staff at all levels." This was one of the conclusions

George Binney drew from analysis of the quality programs of 46 companies across Europe.[7] Only if there are two-way messages can the process be honestly defined as communication.

THE RULES OF THE COMMUNICATIONS GAME[8]

Communications guru Heinz Goldmann has identified the skills of communication as:

♦ ***Empathy.*** *Managers must be able to put themselves in someone else's shoes. They must understand the implications of what they are saying or doing for colleagues, employees, customers and anyone else their behavior affects. The ability to empathize, to understand people, diminishes dramatically when managers have to act outside their protected hierarchical realm.*

♦ ***Commonality.*** *If managers are to communicate they have to find, establish and express a **common denominator** with their target group. There needs to be a bond of solidarity. With growing internationalization, intercultural differences make it even more difficult to build such bonds and communicate effectively. Yet these relationships are essential.*

♦ ***Projection or impact creation.*** *If the delivery is boring then empathy won't help. The impact created is based on projecting a strong message, portraying a powerful personality, impressing by determined (yet acceptable) persuasion. Empathy and projection are not necessarily correlated. Similarly, projection and impact are not automatically helped by using the latest in high-technology devices. In fact, there is an ever-present danger that technology will lead to a greater number of monologues as executives become consumed by what technological gimmickry can do rather than the message they are trying to communicate to their audience. An exhausting parade of charts stifles interest. Also, face-to-face communication is 90 percent more effective than written or printed messages.*

Such two-way communication is vital to achieving the full potential of any such program and to making virtually anything happen in an organization. Participation, empowerment and involvement all revolve around communication.

POSITIVE CONFLICT

"Where there is much desire to learn, there of necessity will be much arguing, much writing, many opinions; for opinions in good men is but knowledge in the making," wrote the English poet John Milton. With a huge range of choices at our disposal and a limited armory of means of delivery, disagreement is inevitable—and vital.

While Jack Welch invests in people, he is not a touchy-feely executive who is fearful of confrontation. He wouldn't have got the nickname Neutron Jack if he was constantly warm and fuzzy. In reality, he suffers fools badly and is impatient if results don't come. He pushes and pushes some more. Anyone who doesn't meet his exacting standards is dispensed with.

What is interesting is that Welch has created a climate of constructive confrontation. That was what Work-Out was chiefly concerned with—people facing up to problems and coming up with ideas. Welch's belief in people and communication means that he is willing to listen to other people's arguments even if they are not in accord with his own feelings.

"Why is there no conflict at this meeting? Something's wrong when there's no conflict," Disney's Michael Eisner said at a conference of his top managers.[9] In a business world characterized by perpetual uncertainty, agreeing to disagree is crucial.

In managing the tensions between doing what the past tells them will yield sustainable (real and acceptable) performance and taking a risk to achieve exceptionally high performance, new leaders must seek out contention and disagreement. They take "yes" for an answer but then ask, "why?"

Seeking out uncertainty goes against the grain. We are as attracted to certainty as presidential candidates are to press conferences. It is, at least in the short term, the surest route to acceptable performance. However, creatively seeking out uncertainty and confrontation may actually offer a more positive and useful way forward.

In his research, Richard Pascale "stumbled" upon a law of cybernetics known as the Law of Requisite Variety. The law states that for any organism to adapt to its external environment, it must incorporate variety. If you reduce variety internally you are less able to deal with it when it comes at you externally. "But how does variety show up in a social system?" asked Pascale. "It shows up as deviance from the norm— other words, as conflict. The problem is that most companies are conflict averse. For many it is associated with wounded egos, harmed relationships and turf wars. Contention is often mistaken as an indicator of mismanagement. The trick is to learn to disagree without being disagreeable and channel this contention as a means of self-questioning and keeping an organization on its toes."[10]

In practice, Pascale believes that 50 percent of the time when contention arises it is smoothed over and avoided. Another 30 percent of the time it leads to nonproductive fighting and no resolution. Only in 20 percent of the cases is contention truly confronted and resolved. "It's ironic," observes Pascale. "A threat that everyone perceives but no one talks about is far more debilitating than a threat that is clearly revealed and resources mobilized to address it. Companies, like people, tend to be as sick as their secrets," says Pascale, who prescribes revealing the "undiscussables" and that "breakdowns" be regarded as a source of learning. Other commentators, such as INSEAD's Manfred Kets de Vries, suggest similar phenomena.

In his 1993 book *Knowledge for Action,* Harvard's Chris Argyris examines the behavior of one of his consultancy clients, itself a consultancy group.[11] The assignment arose when seven successful consultants decided to establish their own company. They hoped that it would be free from the Machiavellian political wrangles they had encountered in other organizations. In practice, their dreams were disappointed. Indeed, by the time Argyris was called in, internal wrangling consumed too many of its productive energies.

The anonymous consultants featured in *Knowledge for Action* were, in fact, falling prey to what Argyris calls *defensive routines.* Faced with a personally threatening problem, the executives were adept at covering it up or bypassing it entirely. Board meetings therefore concentrated on trivial topics. There was always one person keen to avoid discussion of an important issue. Outside the boardroom the big issues were discussed and blame apportioned so that divisions built up relentlessly among the original founders. This approach affected the behavior of the rest of the organization: Others consciously kept infor-

♦ *Invest in communication. Time and money invested in communicating with employees and colleagues are the best investments in short- and long-term corporate performance.*

♦ *Communication is the direct route to innovation. Says Welch: "The bureaucratic paraphernalia that often slows and impedes communications and discourages the innovator and risk-taker has been swept aside; in its place a faster-moving, more action-oriented, and personally more satisfying environment has taken shape."*[13]

♦ *Clear communication creates clear expectations. Clarity of communication is reflected in the clarity of expectations. People at GE know what is expected of them.*

♦ *Communication makes life simple. Jack Welch has a gift for simplifying the complex. "People say, 'Jack, how can you be at NBC; you don't know anything about drama or comedies. . ."* Welch said. *"Well, I can't build a jet engine, either. I can't build a turbine. Our job at GE is to deal with resources—human and financial. The idea of getting great talent, giving them all the support in the world, and letting them run is the whole management philosophy of GE, whether it's in turbines, engines or a network."*[14] *He is adept at making his own job as well as that of the organization as a whole appear blissfully straightforward.*

♦ *Be straight. "Tell them the truth, first because it is the right thing to do and second they'll find out anyway," says Motorola's Paul Galvin. Honest communication is always the best long-term approach despite the lure of short-term temptations.*

mation to a minimum so that executives weren't forced to face up to something new.

The fact that Argyris' client is a group of management consultants helps convey the importance of his message. If highly trained, intelligent executives fall into such traps, what chance have ordinary mortals? For a start, mere mortals have to face up to potential and real problems. They must distrust consensus and embrace contention.

Thriving on conflict is easier said than done. We all like people who agree with us. We like people who have the same perspectives, fears and passions. That is why when managers recruit people they tend to recruit like-minded individuals. Conflict is instinctively buried.

The past has taught us that a narrow band of acceptable behavior is essential. Otherwise we are invaded by uncontrollable renegades and mavericks. Now we need to nurture a much broader band of acceptable behavior. As Don Hambrick noted in a 1987 article, leaders need to surround themselves with people who counter their weaknesses and supplement their strengths.[12] It is notable, for example, that Jack Welch has assembled a group of strong willed executives—including Gary Wendt.

NOTES

1   Author interview.

2   Letter to the Editors, *Fortune*, April 24, 1988.

3   Author interview.

4   Lowe, Janet, *Jack Welch Speaks*, John Wiley & Sons, New York, 1998.

5   Aulleta, Ken, *Three Blind Mice: How the TV Networks Lost Their Way*, Random House, New York, 1991.

6   Lowe, Janet, *Jack Welch Speaks*.

7   Binney, George, "Rising above the bureaucracy of quality," *Directions*, May 1993.

8   Crainer, Stuart (editor), *Financial Times Handbook of Management*, FT/Pitman, London, 1995.

9   Quoted in Huey, J., "Eisner explains everything," *Fortune*, April 1995.

10 Quoted in Crainer, Stuart (editor), *Financial Times Handbook of Management.*

11 Argyris, Chris, *Knowledge for Action*, Jossey-Bass, San Francisco, 1993.

12 Hambrick, D., "The senior management team: a key to success," *California Management Review*, Fall 1987.

13 General Electric Annual Report, 1987.

14 "How GE made NBC No. 1," *Fortune*, February 3, 1997.

Kill Bureaucracy

The organization of offices follows the principle of hierarchy; that is each lower office is under the control and supervision of a higher one.

MAX WEBER

MAGNIFICENT OBSESSIONS

Change programs and corporate revolutions need a rallying cry. At GE, Jack Welch's cry throughout the 1980s and 1990s was to break down boundaries between departments and functions. "Our dream for the 1990s is a boundaryless company, a company where we knock down the walls that separate us from each other on the inside and from our key constituencies on the outside," he said. "The boundaryless company we envision will remove the barriers among engineering, manufacturing, marketing, sales, and customer service; it will recognize no distinction

Welch on the boundaryless organization:

"A boundaryless organization will ignore or erase group labels such as 'management,' 'salaried,' or 'hourly,' which get in the way of people working together."

between domestic and foreign operations—we'll be as comfortable doing business in Budapest and Seoul as we are in Louisiana and Schenectady. A boundaryless organization will ignore or erase group labels such as 'management,' 'salaried,' or 'hourly,' which get in the way of people working together. A boundaryless company will level its external walls as well, reaching out to key suppliers to make them part of a single process in which they and we join hands and intellects in a common purpose—satisfying customers."[1]

There are two aspects to this: Welch's approach to communicating the message and the message itself.

Killing bureaucracy has become a magnificent obsession for Welch and GE. The number of times Welch has repeated the "Kill bureaucracy and eliminate hierarchy" message is beyond calculation. In virtually every interview the subject is returned to.

Here, Welch is treading a very fine line between focus and obsession. Executives commonly wrestle with the demons of obsession. They are obsessed about their sales targets; they are obsessed about reengineering; they are obsessed with corporate politics; or they are obsessed with their latest great idea for boosting performance.

Obsession is one of the unspoken facts of business life. Managers frequently have to be obsessed to succeed—or even obsessed with success. The business world does not, however, have a monopoly on obsession. Educational systems encourage children to be obsessive and sport is dominated by obsessives who think of nothing else but crossing the line first, jumping higher or hitting the ball harder. Coaches encourage this form of obsession (though they call it "focus") in the same way as a boss is liable to encourage the obsessive traits of a young manager who works 16 hours a day and lives for the business.

"There is culturally acceptable obsession—musicians who practice 12 hours a day—and unacceptable obsession," says Ashridge Management College's Phil Hodgson. "In organizational life we expect and demand obsessional behavior from managers. Yet, later in their careers if they take up more senior positions we expect them to throw off obsessional qualities to adopt a wider view."[2]

All-pervasive obsession is regarded as a good thing. There is a fundamental belief that obsession motivates. The chief executive works days, nights and weekends not simply because this is what gets the work done; he or she believes that this is what motivates others to do the same. Leading by obsessional example means that managers work longer and longer hours. The question of whether these extra hours make them more productive is rarely addressed.

Even so, obsession is sometimes essential. If you are starting your own business, tepid enthusiasm is not enough. You have to live for your bright idea. The bank manager demands obsessive commitment and belief that the business will work. Nothing less will do.

Similarly, if you are leading a Total Quality Management initiative, keenness is inadequate. Obsessional behavior can set new standards of customer service. Companies such as McDonald's and Marks & Spencer are built around an obsessive commitment to giving customers quality service.

Welch's obsession with boundaries and hierarchies is a common one. His current obsession is with breaking down functional divides. At one company a senior manager developed an obsession with eliminating long-established barriers. To prove his point, on a walk around the company's factory he asked everyone he met what they did to "functional silos." The replies were uniformly aggressive. His obsession had gotten an important point across.

The trouble is that obsession can lead managers and their businesses down potentially costly blind alleys. Henry Ford fervently believed that all people wanted was a low-cost, uniform car. He delivered it to great acclaim and then sat back as General Motors sped past with constantly changing models in different colors. Ford's obsession was too rigid and unbending to take his company forward. Similarly, IBM developed an obsessional belief in mainframes and then stood bemused as upstarts eroded its markets.

Any psychologist will point out that obsession is dangerously unhealthy. As a result, managers are engaged in a precarious balancing act. When does the dealer who is energetically and constantly pulling off deals become an obsessive Gordon Ghekko-like figure, discarding any pretense of ethical behavior? When do commitment and enthusiasm become obsession?

Ashridge's Phil Hodgson believes there is a dividing line between commitment (which he characterizes as healthy and outward-looking) and obsession (unhealthy and inward-looking). "If obsessive managers took a step back it would be easy for them to recognize the unhealthy side of the obsession. It dominates their life to the detriment of family, friends and fun," says Hodgson. "Obsession is a potent force which needs to be harnessed to the organizational good rather than being allowed to gather pace by itself. Managers spend huge amounts of energy in obsessive search of promotions and engaging in corporate politics. If this energy was set free and channeled, a potentially enormous corporate and individual resource would be unleashed."

Whether it is used to convince a bank manager reticent about a loan or to drive through a program of radical change, the power of obsessional behavior cannot be doubted. The only doubt lies in our ability to use it to positive ends.

THE BUREAUCRATIC MODEL

The German sociologist Max Weber argued that the most efficient form of organization resembled a machine. It was characterized by strict rules, controls and hierarchies and driven by bureaucracy. This Weber termed the "rational-legal model." At the opposite extreme were the "charismatic" model and the "traditional" model. In the charismatic model, a single dominant figure ran the organization. Weber dismissed this as a viable long-term solution. Once again Weber was the first to discuss a viable phenomenon and examine its ramifications. History bears Weber out. An organization built around a single charismatic figure is unsustainable in the long term.

The final organizational form Weber identified was the traditional model where things are done as they always have been done, such as in family firms in which power is passed down from one generation to the next.

If it was pure efficiency you required there was, said Weber, only one choice: "Experience tends universally to show that the purely bureaucratic type of administrative organization—that is, the monocratic variety of bureaucracy—is, from a purely technical point of view, capable of attaining the highest degree of efficiency and is in this sense formally the most rational known means of carrying our imperative control over human beings," Weber wrote. "It is superior

*to any other form in precision, in stability, in the stringency
of its discipline, and in its reliability. It thus makes possible
a particularly high degree of calculability of results for the
heads of the organization and for those acting in relation
to it. It is finally superior both in intensive efficiency and in
the scope of its operations and is formally capable of appli-
cation to all kinds of administrative tasks."*

*Modern commentators usually cannot resist the urge to
scoff at Weber's insights. The bureaucratic business world
he described was denuded of life and inspiration. Yet it
largely came to pass.*

*If you wish for further proof, look at the success of Scott
Adams' Dilbert, based on the mundanity and regularity of
corporate life.*

*The bureaucratic model as outlined by Weber to a large
extent became reality. It was an undoubtedly narrow way
of doing things and one that seems out of step with our
times. Yet in the early part of the twentieth century, it was
a plausible and effective means of doing business. Like all
great insights, it worked, for a while at least. At GE it
worked especially well.*

COOKING GEESE

Well-run and successful though GE was in the generations prior to Jack Welch's arrival as CEO, the company had erected a formidable network of systems and
layers of management to ensure that it was performing. It was bureaucratic but rational.

GE was not alone. Its array of managerial layers
and internal systems was generally typical of how large
companies had evolved. Indeed, complexity and
growth were usually regarded as inextricably linked.
Welch explains: "Picture a building. Companies all

added floors as they got bigger. Size adds floors. Complexity adds walls. We all build departments—transportation departments, research departments. That's complexity. That's walls. The job all of us have in business is to flatten the building and break down the walls. If we do that, we will be getting more people coming up with more ideas for the action items that a business needs to work with."[3]

Welch discovered a lot of walls. "As I went to bigger pieces of GE, I found bigger bureaucracies—layers and all that stuff—and it wasn't friendly. Business was very serious—turf—boxes," he says. "Business isn't that. Business is ideas and fun and excitement and celebrations, all those things."[4]

The targets of Jack Welch's obsession became the devilish twins of bureaucracy and hierarchy.

Throughout the 1980s, Welch decimated hierarchies. "During the 80s we eliminated layer after layer of management. We took down wall after wall separating functions. We reduced staff—the checkers, kibitzers. As we did this, we found, first at the business leadership level and then down in the organization, that people who were given space—trusted, allowed to make their own decisions—worked harder at making sure they made good decisions."[5]

The number of management layers was trimmed from 29 to 6. Those bearing the brunt were the middle-ranking executives, the checkers in suits. According to Tom Peters, "Middle managers are cooked geese." Welch cooked a great many.

KILL BUREAUCRACY

Welch has been proved right. Big but not laden with hierarchies, GE is the new organizational model. This model is characterized by:

♦ **Speed.** *Traditional large organizations were slow. Decisions emerged. GE is shaped to move quickly and make decisions speedily. "Speed is everything. It is the indispensable ingredient in competitiveness. Speed keeps businesses—and people—young. It's addictive, and it's a profoundly American taste we need to cultivate," says Welch.[6]*

♦ **Informality.** *It was once insisted that McKinsey consultants wore hats. No more. Pointless formality makes people uncomfortable and gets in the way of the real work. Says Welch: "The story about GE that hasn't been told is the value of an informal place. I think it's a big thought. I don't think people have ever figured out that being informal is a big deal."[7]*

♦ **Ideas, not management layers.** *"The hero is the one with the ideas," says Jack Welch.[8] Businesses are driven forward by bright ideas, not additional layers of supervision.*

♦ **Sharing information.** *"Boundaryless behavior is a way of life here. People really do take ideas from A to B," says Welch. "And if you take an idea and share it, you are rewarded. In the old culture, if you had an idea you'd keep it. Sharing it with someone else would have been stupid, because the bureaucracy would have made him the hero, not you."[9] Information shared—internally and externally with customers and suppliers—is information multiplied.*

It worked. By 1987, his success in ridding the company of over-weighty bureaucracy was being celebrated. "Like him or not, Jack Welch has succeeded in sweeping a major American company clean of the bureaucratic excesses of the past and transforming a paternalistic culture into one that pits winning in the marketplace above all other concerns," said *BusinessWeek*. "Like it or not, the management styles of more U.S. companies are going to look a lot more like GE."[10]

NOTES

1 Welch, Jack, "Today's leaders look to tomorrow," *Fortune*, March 26, 1990.

2 Author interview.

3 "Create a company of ideas," *Fortune*, December 30, 1991.

4 Lowe, Janet, *Jack Welch Speaks*, John Wiley & Sons, New York, 1998.

5 Lowe, Janet, *Jack Welch Speaks*.

6 Mitchell, Russell and Dobrzynski, Judith, "GE's Jack Welch: how good a manager is he?" *Business Week*, December 14, 1987.

7 Speech, 1992 New Englander of the Year Award, November 11, 1992.

8 Byrne, John, "How Jack Welch runs GE," *Business Week*, June 8, 1998.

9 Day, Charles R. and LaBarre, Polly, "GE: Just your everyday $60 billion family grocery store," *Industry Week*, May 2, 1994.

10 Quoted in Jackson, T. and Gowers, A., "Big enough to make mistakes," *Financial Times*, December 21, 1995.

Stick Around

The day of combination is here to stay.
Individualism has gone, never to return.

John D. Rockefeller

CORPORATE MAN LIVES ON

One of the great books of management literature is William Whyte's 1956 classic, *The Organization Man*, with its poignant descriptions of corporate life. "The fundamental premise of the new model executive ... is, simply, that the goals of the individual and the goals of the organization will work out to be one and the same. The young men have no cynicism about the 'system,' and very little skepticism— they don't see it as something to be bucked, but as something to be co-operated with . . . they have an implicit faith that the organization will be as interested in making use of their best qualities as they are themselves, and this, with equanimity, they can entrust the resolution of their destiny to the organization . . . the average young man cherishes the idea that his relationship with the organization is to be for keeps." Whyte described a world in which the organization choked inspiration in the name of efficiency. The individual was subsumed under the bureaucratic machine.

The corporate person described by Whyte and commonplace in postwar corporations was cool under pressure, reliable and ready to spend his or her life with a single organization. Implicit to such careers was the understanding that loyalty and solid performance brought job security. This was mutually beneficial. The executive gained a respectable income and a high degree of security. The company gained loyal, hard-working executives.

This unspoken pact became known as the psychological contract. The originator of the phrase was the social psychologist Ed Schein of MIT. Schein's interest in the employee–employer relationship developed during the late 1950s. Schein noted the similarities between the brainwashing of POWs he had witnessed during the Korean War and the corporate indoctrination carried out by the likes of GE at Crotonville and IBM in its training centers.

As Schein's link with brainwashing suggests, there was more to the psychological contract than a cozy, mutually beneficial deal. It raised a number of issues.

First, the psychological contract was built around loyalty. "The most important single contribution required of an executive, certainly the most universal qualification, is loyalty [allowing] domination by the organization personality," noted Chester Barnard in *The Functions of the Executive* (1938). (The word "domination" suggests which way Barnard saw the balance of power falling.) While loyalty is a positive quality, it can easily become blind. What if the corporate strategy is wrong or the company is engaged in unlawful or immoral acts? Also, there is the question of loyalty to what values? Thirty years ago, corporate values were assumed rather than explored.

The second issue raised by the psychological contract was that of perspectives. With careers neatly mapped out, executives were hardly encouraged to look over the corporate parapets to seek out broader viewpoints. The corporation became a self-contained and self-perpetuating world supported by a complex array of checks, systems, and hierarchies. The company was right. Customers, who existed in the ethereal world outside the organization, were often regarded as peripheral. In the fifties, sixties and seventies, no executive ever lost a job by delivering poor quality or indifferent service. "Jobs for life" was the refrain and, to a large extent for executives, the reality.

Clearly, such an environment was not conducive to the fostering of dynamic risk takers. The psychological contract rewarded the steady foot soldier, the safe pair of hands. It was hardly surprising therefore that when she came to examine corporate life for the first time in her 1977 book, *Men and Women of the Corporation*, Rosabeth Moss Kanter found that the central characteristic expected of a manager was "dependability."

The reality was that the psychological contract placed a premium on loyalty rather than ability and allowed a great many poor performers to seek out corporate havens. It was also significant that the psychological contract was regarded as the preserve of management. Lower down in the hierarchy, people were hired and fired with abandon.

As the use of the past tense suggests, in recent years there have been radical changes to the psycho-

> *"It was once the case that unless you were caught with your hand in the till, or publicly slandered your boss, you could count on a job for life in many large companies."*

logical contract between employers and employees. The rash of downsizing in the 1980s and 1990s marked the end of the psychological contract that had existed for decades.

Managerial life is no longer straightforward. Dependable at what? Loyal to whom? Listen to Gary Hamel, coauthor of *Competing for the Future:* "It was once the case that unless you were caught with your hand in the till, or publicly slandered your boss, you could count on a job for life in many large companies. Loyalty was valued more than capability, and there was always a musty corner where mediocrity could hide. Entitlement produced a reasonably malleable workforce, and dependency enforced a begrudging kind of loyalty. That was then, this is now."[1]

Expectations have now changed on both sides. Employers no longer wish to make commitments—even implicit ones—to long-term employment. The emphasis is on flexibility. On the other side, employees are keen to develop their skills and take charge of their own careers. Employability is the height of fashion.

As a result, the new psychological contract is more likely to be built on developing skills than on blind loyalty. The logic is that if a company invests in an individual's development, the employee will become more loyal. The trouble is that the employee also becomes more employable by other companies.

In effect the balance has shifted. The original and long-standing psychological contract created an artificial balance based on inefficient behavior. Its emphasis was on loyalty and reliability rather than performance. Performance was assumed. Downsizing and the decimation of middle management swung the pendulum toward corporations. Managerial job security was overturned. Now, it is employees who potentially hold the balance of power. In the age of flexible employment, downsizing and career management, loyalty is increasingly elusive as managers flit from job to job, company to company.

The old psychological contract, with its inherent safety and clarity, is now being reevaluated as a corporate nirvana. We never had it so good, some say. The trouble is that the concept of jobs for life was largely a mirage. Companies may have been prepared to stick with the same managers throughout their careers, but often the companies themselves didn't last. (Whether this was due to the inertia of management is open to debate.) Research repeatedly shows that companies don't last very long. One survey of corporate life expectancy in Japan and Europe estimated that 12.5 years is the average life expectancy of all firms. London Business School's Arie de Geus estimates that the average life expectancy of a multinational corporation is 40 to 50 years.

The ebb and flow of corporate life means that the traditional psychological contract is unlikely to return. However, there will always be a psychological contract between employer and employee. In any employment deal, each side carries expectations, aspirations and an understanding, which may be right or wrong, of the expectations and aspirations of the other side. The new challenge is for both sides to make the psychological contract an explicit arrangement.

JACK WELCH: CORPORATE MAN

In the era of career management and employability, loyalty to the corporation is decidedly unfashionable. There is the feeling, when you hear of people who have been with a company for a long time, that they have been shackled. You tend to wonder what might have happened if they had been set loose.

Lurking behind such responses is the now commonplace assumption that being a corporate man or woman is a bad thing, that unswerving loyalty diminishes people instead of enriching. Here we are wrong. Jack Welch is a one-company man. For Welch and many thousands of others, loyalty is not cheaply bought. He remains curious and questioning even now, nearing the end of his corporate career.

Arie de Geus has studied the relationship between companies and employees in *The Living Company*. He provides the new deal: Contemporary corporate man or woman must understand that the corporation will, and must, change and it can only change if its community of people changes also. Individuals must change and the way they change is through learning. As a result, de Geus believes that senior executives must dedicate a great deal of time to nurturing their people. He recalls spending around a quarter of his time on the development and placement of people. Jack Welch claims to spend half of his time on such issues.

The corporate person lives on, but only by learning and questioning, developing as his or her career unfolds. Welch argues that experience and the security of being able to make mistakes are important to personal development. Says Welch: "A GE chief executive doesn't have to serve 15 to 20 years, but I think you need to serve ten years, otherwise you get these insane moves. I've seen some companies like that. During my time as CEO, there have been five CEOs in some places; six in some places. You show up at meetings, and there's another one there. When the people are only there a couple of years, everybody's trying to do something, make their stamp quickly. And so I think you should live with your errors. Work on them. Business is a series of processes; they're not perfect."[2] Development is all. Imperfection means you can do better next time.

Flaunt your imperfection:

"I think you should live with your errors. Work on them. Business is a series of processes; they're not perfect."

MAXIMIZING EXPERIENCE

Managerial potential used to be considered the ability to "get on" or get along in the organization, the ability to lubricate the wheels of corporate culture. It was about power and politics as much as anything else. Organizations are now beginning to see that potential is as much the ability to learn, grow and change, while performance is a separate dimension.

According to Randall P. White of Greensboro, NC-based RPW Executive Development and coauthor of *Breaking the Glass Ceiling* and *The Future of Leadership*, to compete effectively, organizations have begun consciously to use job assignments to develop two groups of managers. One group, currently the recipient of most developmental opportunities are the high-potential managers, those likely to become future leaders of the organization. The second group, the organization's solid citizens, comprises the bulk of managerial talent in large organizations. But as organizations become flatter and these technical or functional managers plateau at earlier ages, organizations need to use on-the-job development to keep them challenged as well. Using job assignments strategically to match the developmental needs of the individual and the business will have positive benefits for the organization.

The idea that one learns from experience is neither novel nor a revelation.[3] In the past several years organizations have started looking at the types of experiences available for developing future leaders. This is an outgrowth of a rediscovery that experience is an invaluable, if not the best, teacher of leadership.

There is a need to understand the types of experiences from which people tend to learn and to understand the types of learning that result from various experiences. Companies also need to target specific experiences as developmental opportunities and in turn practice good stewardship of those opportunities; and help candidates learn from developmental experiences through coaching both prior to and after the experience.

In his research, White found that job assignments—fixing broken businesses, moving from line to staff jobs, starting new businesses, being on a special project or task force, or managing large scale and scope—were most often mentioned as triggers for learning, growth and change. Executives reported significant learning experiences stemming from hardships and learning from other people, both the revered and the hated, mostly bosses in their past. But when closely scrutinized, the greatest point of developmental leverage involves the assignments an organization has to offer.

White found that there are different challenges involved in each assignment type. Fixing a business had different leadership challenges than starting a business. So different types of assignments were found to teach different lessons. For example, starting a new business tends to teach standing alone, being in charge, discovering what one really wants to do, getting cooperation from people one has no control over and understanding what makes other people tick. Special projects and task force assignments, on the other hand, teach very different lessons of comfort with uncertainty, knowing how to work with executives and how they think, and negotiation skills.

As the developmental potential of the job increases (for example, it has many elements that are new or there are unfamiliar skills to be applied) the risk to the business (the risk of failure resulting in lost time, money, productivity, etc.) likewise increases. Since most businesses operate in a risk-averse or at best in a balanced risk-taking stance, many potential developmental assignments go to candidates who can already do what is required to get the job done. For example if there are major problems at one of the company's plants, someone will be sent who has fixed things before. This practice often results in an organization developing a cadre of single-experience leaders—leaders who know how to fix things but not how to run a smoothly operating business. When there are no longer those situations facing the organization, the single-experience leader becomes obsolete, a loss for the organization as well as the individual.

A more complete determination of the developmental potential of an assignment then rests with evaluating the abilities and track record of the candidate against the types of learning likely from that assignment. In other words, the developmental potential of the job changes with the candidate for the job. Obviously for a candidate who can already do the job there is little or no potential for further development. For someone who cannot perform, the developmental potential and concomitant risk to the business are very high. So organizations have to provide support for development via coaching, counseling and mentoring.

There are some important caveats to using assignments for development:

♦ Individuals who are chosen for a developmental assignment ought to be told why they are getting the assignment. Furthermore, some support system ought to be put in place.

♦ Developmental moves won't fix every weakness, nor will they build leadership in everyone.

♦ Most organizations don't have enough big assignments to develop all the leaders they'll need in the future. But there are ways to develop people that don't involve sending them to start an operation in Warsaw, Poland or to shut down a factory in Tanzania. Developing them in place by providing additional (and often targeted) responsibilities can provide challenges.[4]

Every assignment is potentially developmental for someone. A critical step in the process is to involve the target of development—the individual—in the process.

STICK AROUND

Top jobs need new skills. In fact, all jobs need new skills all the time:

Says Stella Sinden of GHN Executive Coaching: "Making the transition to becoming a first rate director requires skills in managing people. If you look at boards they are peopled by individuals who tend to be aggressive and successful. They have risen through organizations because they negate the competition. Suddenly they find themselves in the boardroom and have to understand and take on completely different roles. They have to adapt their behavior in new contexts. They have to be responsive, take lateral perspectives, understand opposing positions."[5]

♦ *Learn from experience. Jack Welch ensured that he gained a wide range of experience in his early years with GE. He got businesses off the ground and turned around those that were ailing. He developed new skills.*

♦ *Give people time to make mistakes, learn from them and put them right. Our short-term business culture tends to expect a never-ending cycle of success. When bosses screw up they are fired. What if they were given the opportunity to sort things out, to rectify their errors? This would give them long-term confidence. Indeed, it could focus their attention on long-term growth rather than short-term survival.*

♦ *Developing people is the new contract. The new psychological contract is driven by development. Companies must develop their people in order to recruit and retain the best people for the job.*

NOTES

1 Hamel, Gary, Foreword to *The Financial Times Handbook of Management* (ed. Crainer, S.), FT/Pitman, London, 1995.

2 Lowe, Janet, *Jack Welch Speaks*, John Wiley, New York, 1998.

3 See for example McCall, M.W., Jr, Lombardo, M.M. and Morrison, A.M., *The Lessons of Experience: How Successful Executives Develop on the Job*, Lexington Books, Lexington, MA, 1988; and Morrison, A.M., White, R.P. and Van Velsor, E., *Breaking the Glass Ceiling: Can Women Reach the Top of America's Largest Corporations?* (Revised edition) Addison Wesley, Reading, MA, 1992, 1994.

4 See, for example, Lombardo, M.M. and Eichinger, R.W., *Eighty-Eight Assignments for Development in Place: Enhancing the Development Challenge of Existing Jobs*, Center for Creative Leadership (Technical Report 136), Greensboro, 1989; and Eichinger, R.W. and Lombardo, M.M., *Twenty-Two Ways to Develop Leadership in Staff Managers*, Center for Creative Leadership (Technical Report 144), Greensboro, 1990.

5 Author interview.

Manage the Corner Store

GE: Just your average everyday $60 billion family grocery store

INDUSTRY WEEK HEADLINE

THE BIGGEST CORNER STORE
IN THE WORLD

People have searched high and low for what makes Jack Welch tick. They have analyzed his management style and the GE culture from every angle. They have analyzed and then analyzed some more. Most end up writing wish lists. "There are many characteristics that have made Jack Welch famous, notorious, feared, respected, and admired," writes Adrian Slywotsky in *Value Migration*. "He is hard-driving and focused. He creates a simple and consistent strategic message that is communicated clearly to the organization. He is a consummate high-level marketer. And an extraordinary creator of value and value growth."[1]

Forbes identified the secret of Welch's success as, "Not a series of brilliant insights or bold gambles, but a fanatical attention to detail."[2] Another book noted,

"Welch inspires remarkable affection, respect and enthusiasm among GE's managers," going on to quote a GE executive: "He is incredibly smart. He can think strategically, but he is also good with people, with deals, with organization, with politics. He can make the sort of inputs to guys running the business that only an outsider who has a really informed view can make."[3]

Renaissance man or not, Jack Welch keeps his feet on the ground. He runs GE like no one else could, but he doesn't act like a smart-ass CEO who knows it all. He is doing his job the best he can. Period.

Welch keeps things in perspective by regarding GE as a simple business. It may have sales measured in billions of dollars and market domination and global success, but it is still a business and, as Jack Welch repeatedly observes, business is not rocket science. "What's important at the grocery store is just as important in engines or medical systems," says Welch. "If the customer isn't satisfied, if the stuff is getting stale, if the shelf isn't right, or if the offerings aren't right, it's the same thing. You manage it like a small organization. You don't get hung up on zeroes."[4]

MANAGE CASH FLOW

Ask any owner of a small business what the biggest problem is and the inevitable answer is: cash flow. Yet if you go to larger companies, cash flow is rarely men-

---

tioned. Somewhere along the line it slips from the managerial agenda. Managers in big companies tend to spend their time talking about strategy rather than the more mundane issue of how much money the company actually has as of that moment. Indeed, cash flow is often poorly monitored and, sometimes, little understood in the context of a big corporation.

Welch on measurements:

"The three most important things you need to measure in a business are customer satisfaction, employee satisfaction, and cash flow."

Jack Welch has returned cash flow to center stage. "Too often we measure everything and understand nothing. The three most important things you need to measure in a business are customer satisfaction, employee satisfaction, and cash flow. If you're growing customer satisfaction, your global market share is sure to grow, too. Employee satisfaction feeds you productivity, quality, pride, and creativity. And cash flow is the pulse—the key vital sign of a company."[5]

Cash flow is concerned with making the cash work. "Cash is a fact, profit is an opinion," argues Alfred Rappaport of Northwestern University's Kellogg School of Management. Rappaport is one of the champions of shareholder value, a fashionable theory that basically applies cash flow theories to large organizations.

Welch's faith in cash flow goes against some of the first principles of corporate life. Most obviously it calls into question the accounting model of measuring corporate performance. Erwin Scholtz of Ashridge Management College is among those who pour a measure of scorn on the traditional accounting model whose currency is profits rather than cash. Scholtz suggests that the accounting model is incomplete (because it does not account for the full cost of capital); complex (it uses multiple performance measures); inconsistent (producing conflicting signals); incorrect (because accounting conventions can distort true economic performance); and ineffective (because it is often disconnected from the management systems and operational drivers of the business).

Welch is concerned with the nitty-gritty: cash flow; goods in; goods out. "In manufacturing, A players consider inventory an embarrassment, especially with a whiff of deflation in the air," he wrote in his letter to GE employees in the company's 1997 annual report.

In his dedication to cash flow and reducing inventory and improving processes, Welch is once again ahead of the game. Mercer Management Consulting has studied inventory and accounts receivables practices in a variety of industries. "While operating costs have been pounded over the last 15 years in the process industries, the studies point conclusively to an untapped opportunity to improve cash flow, reduce costs, and increase return on capital employed through aggressive working capital management," says Scott Setrakian, lead partner of Mercer's energy and process industries consulting practice.

Working capital is frequently overlooked in corporate ledger books, Setrakian says, even though it can constitute a sizeable chunk: Up to 20 percent of total capital in process industries is frequently tied up in inventory, receivables and payables. "Working capital touches many points in the company, making optimization particularly difficult," explains Setrakian. "Product and information flows, as well as customer relationships, must be co-ordinated across divisions. But the rewards of liberating capital can be considerable."[6]

However, the integrative nature of working capital resists A-level management. Due to the complexities, companies seldom have accurate metrics in place to measure working capital levels, much less to hold management accountable for its maintenance. The Mercer study found that the most commonly used metric to track receivables—day's sales outstanding (DSO)—is often seriously misleading. "Clearly," says Setrakian, "execution presents numerous issues and challenges, both with the customer and internally. Nonetheless, as customer requirements become more sophisticated, these links will be the hallmarks of a successful competitor." This will require overcoming the internal barriers—clearly the hallmark of A management.

MANAGE THE CORNER STORE

+ *Watch the cash.* Applying cash flow management to a business, any business must make sense. It also has the advantage of being widely understood.

+ *Keep the parameters of performance simple.* Nothing fancy. Welch stresses simple measures of corporate performance. He doesn't tend to mention Return on Capital or other fashionable theories. Instead, his parameters of success are cash, service and business basics like inventory.

+ *Management is management.* Whether you are managing a grocery store or a conglomerate, the basics are the same. Forget this at your peril.

NOTES

1   Slywotzky, Adrian, *Value Migration*, Harvard Business School Press, Boston, MA, 1996.

2   Conlin, Michelle, "Revealed at last: the secret of Jack Welch's success," *Forbes*, January 26, 1998.

3   Campbell, Andrew, Goold, Michael and Alexander, Marcus, *Corporate-Level Strategy*, John Wiley & Sons, New York, 1994.

4   Byrne, John, "How Jack Welch runs GE," *Business Week*, June 8, 1998.

5   Tichy, Noel and Sherman, Stratford, *Control Your Own Destiny or Someone Else Will*, Doubleday Currency, New York, 1993.

6   "Process industries face working capital challenge," *Mercer Management Briefs*, April 1998.

How Long Can Jack Welch Be Effective?

People who are highly successful tend to find it extremely hard to acknowledge when their powers begin to wane. Sports stars notoriously carry on for one more fight, one more race, another tournament, when their skills are rapidly disappearing.

Leaders face similar problems. Winston Churchill was a dynamic war leader, but his period of office during peacetime tarnished rather than enhanced his image and reputation. It is not that skills vanish overnight, but often the skills that make leaders successful in a particular organization outlive their usefulness. The charismatic leader who creates a fast-growing, dynamic organization is rarely the person who should continue to lead it when it becomes a giant multinational. Indeed, the charismatic leader is now commonly regarded with some skepticism. Peter Drucker acknowledges the importance of authority in management, but suggests that charismatic leaders are often blinkered by an illusion of their own infallibility. Believing themselves infallible, they become inflexible and unable to cope with a changing environment.

Being aware of the time limitations is an important factor identified by a number of leaders. For some, like BA's Colin Marshall, it is regarded as something requiring constant vigilance. In an interview with this author, Colin said, "The problem commonly encountered by leaders—in whatever field—is that the length of time they have spent in office leads to them being cut off from reality. As a result, they fail to recognize their faults and mistakes. Leaders have to be wary of longevity." Sir Colin pointed to Robert Townsend's suggestion that no one should be in one position for more than five years. It is not a view Sir Colin holds, but one that serves as a warning: "You must watch for signs of egotism and a lack of willingness to acknowledge mistakes."

Jack Welch has been at the top for much longer than five years. He appears comfortable there, more so than virtually anyone else who has ever been a CEO. He has worked on through the hard times of the 1980s and through a heart operation. He is due to retire at the end of the year 2000. The signs are that GE's tradition of managing succession will allow him to pass on the reins seamlessly. The juggernaut will not grind to a halt. Welch is steeped in GE from his head to his toes, but he is not GE. The GE culture is too robust and carefully constructed to fall to the ambition or ego of one person. It was always so. Jack Welch has simply made it more so.

His successor will have a hard act to follow. GE continues to break records. Asian economic turmoil and a rising dollar have had little effect on the company's financial performance. Future prosperity appears assured. But the great lesson of Jack Welch's career should not be forgotten: Change when the going is good. Change now to get ahead of the competition. If you delay you will be forced to change.

How to Manage
the Jack Welch Way

J ack Welch is unique and uniquely successful. But there are some universally applicable rules that can be extracted from the story of his career:

1. Make your job description easily understood . . . and then tell everyone

"My job is to put the best people on the biggest opportunities and the best allocation of dollars in the right place," says Welch.[1] Simple, really.

2. Revolutionize, don't tinker

Incremental change is tempting but can be self-defeating. Big leaps are better.

3. Change continually

Complacency is the biggest corporate killer. Move, then move again.

4. Think positive

Jack Welch believes that everything can and will be improved. "Productivity is not the squeezing out of a rag. Productivity is the belief that there's an infinite capacity to improve anything."[2]

5. Surround yourself with quality

You may look good surrounded by yes-people. But Jack Welch has surrounded himself with formidable executives, people like Gary Wendt at GE Capital and Robert Wright at NBC.

6. Learn, always

Whether you stay with one company or a dozen, your progress can only be measured by your learning, not your salary.

7. Keep it simple, stupid

Whatever you are doing, keep it simple: simple communication, simple measurements, simple aims, simple systems.

8. Look after your people

Look after your people and the company will look after itself. Talk to the people and develop them constantly.

9. Plan succession

Tomorrow is your responsibility.

10. Make mistakes

Everyone does. You either admit it and learn from it or carry on, oblivious. Being oblivious is the route to oblivion.

NOTES

1   Quoted in van Clieaf, M.S., "Executive resource and succession planning," *American Journal of Management Development*, Vol. 1, No. 2, 1995.

2   Day, Charles R. and LaBarre, Polly, "GE: just your average $60 billion family grocery store," *Industry Week*, May 3, 1994.

Further Reading

Lowe, Janet, *Jack Welch Speaks*, John Wiley & Sons, New York, 1998.

Slater, Robert, *Jack Welch and the GE Way*, McGraw-Hill, New York, 1998.

Tichy, Noel M. and Sherman, Stratford, *Control Your Destiny or Someone Else Will*, Doubleday Currency, New York, 1993.

Index